Walk Lo

G000147154

Contents

Getting around London is easy – and if you walk it, it is also a lot of fun. Walking gives you the chance to truly appreciate the wealth of historic and modern-day sites the city has to offer that are missed when you travel underground, or the nooks and crannies that you can't explore if you're on a bus.

The illustrated maps in Walk London guide you through 15 routes that take in many of the city's best-loved must-see icons, but also encourage you to stop and look at things a little out of the ordinary or less well known.

The walks vary in length from approximately 1 to 5½ miles (1.5 to 9 kilometres). How long they take depends on how long you've got and how many of the attractions you want to spend time at, so is something you may want to decide before you set off. You'll even find that entry to many visitor sites is absolutely free – but do check opening dates and times beforehand; contact details are given in the Visitor Information section at the end of this guide.

Look for the green arrow ➡ which indicates the start point on each walk map. Each one starts and ends at an Underground or railway station but if you only have time to do part of a walk it is usually possible to finish at a different station as shown on the maps.

Love London? Live it. Walk it.

WALK 1 – Exploring the Embankment

DISTANCE: 3½ miles (5.5 kilometres)
START: Westminster Underground
END: St Paul's Underground

Exit Westminster Underground following the signs to the Houses of Parliament and soaring before you is one of London's most famous landmarks – Big Ben. The tower that houses the great bell known as Big Ben is officially called the Westminster Clock Tower.

Big Ben

1 Head away from the river up Bridge Street where you will see Parliament Square and a statue of Winston Churchill ahead of you. Go left here for the main entrance to the Houses of Parliament where you can attend debates and, usually by prior arrangement, tour the buildings and even climb Big Ben.

A royal palace was originally established here by King Canute on the marshy ground on the banks of the River Thames in the 11th century. The official name for the Houses of Parliament is the New Palace of Westminster. These fine buildings were designed by Charles Barry as the result of a competition, following a fire in 1834 that demolished most of the Old Palace.

2 Return to Parliament Square, turning left for a magnificent view of the west front of Westminster Abbey. Above this entrance are ten statues of 20th-century martyrs. There is much to see in the abbey, including the Grave of the Unknown Warrior, where a solider was buried on 11 November 1920 to honour all those who died unidentified in the First World War.

As you leave Westminster Abbey, on your right is St Margaret's Church, originally built as a place of worship

Gilbert and Sullivan

The charming monument to Arthur Sullivan in Victoria Embankment Gardens depicts the beautiful Muse of Song and Harmony as she weeps for her loss.

The pedestal on which Sullivan's bust sits bears a poignant inscription from *The Yeoman of the Guard*, penned by his musical partner W.S. Gilbert:

Is life a boon
If so it must befall
That death, whene'er he call
Must call too soon

for the servants of the monks of Westminster. Since 1614 it has been the parish church of the House of Commons; Winston Churchill's wedding took place here in 1908.

Cross to Parliament Square where alongside Churchill are statues of such greats as Nelson Mandela, Abraham Lincoln and Benjamin Disraeli.

Now head back towards the river and Westminster Bridge. Cross the road opposite Thomas Thornycroft's bronze masterpiece of Boudicca, commissioned by Prince Albert, Queen Victoria's consort, and completed in 1905.

3 Go down the steps to Victoria Embankment, with the River Thames on your right. A short distance along you come to the imposing Battle of Britain monument. This granite structure, with bronze-relief depictions of scenes from the 1940 battle, honours 'The Few' – airmen of the RAF referred to in Churchill's stirring speech: 'Never in the field of human conflict was so much owed by so many to so few.' A little further on is the RAF memorial topped with a golden eagle, unveiled in 1923 to commemorate the airmen who died in the First World War.

Continue along the Embankment to Golden Jubilee Bridges, two footbridges opened in 2003. Between these and Waterloo Bridge is Cleopatra's Needle. This obelisk, guarded by two sphinxes, dates from *c*.1460 BC and was transported from Egypt to this spot in 1878 as a memorial to Nelson and Abercromby for their victories over Napoleon in Egypt.

Westminster Abbey

4 Cross the road opposite Cleopatra's Needle where there is a monument to the British nation from the people of Belgium. Just beyond, go through the entrance to Victoria Embankment Gardens. Go left and just past the café and a statue of poet Robert Burns is York Water Gate; built in 1626 it stands on what was once the edge of the river before the land was reclaimed by the Embankment. The gate was an entry to York House which stood on this site.

If you leave the gardens a few steps beyond York Water Gate and turn right into Villiers Street you can visit Gordon's, the oldest wine bar in London, established in 1890. The building was home to Samuel Pepys in the 1680s and Rudyard Kipling lived here in the 1890s; it was in a room over the bar that he wrote his first novel, *The Light that Failed*.

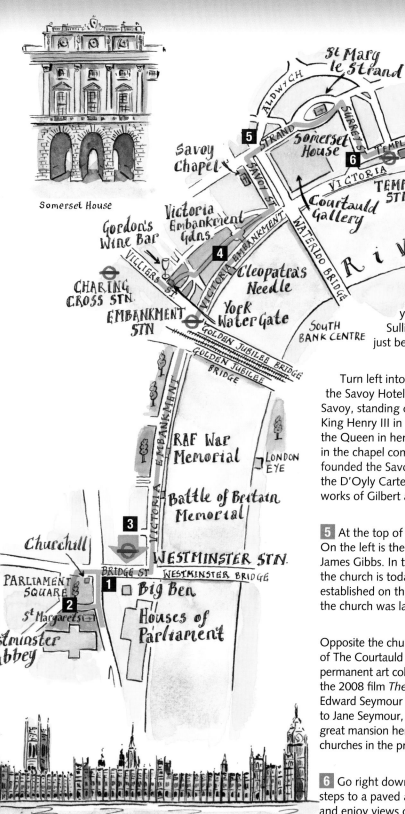

Somerset House

Houses of Parliament

Back in Embankment Gardens, retrace your steps, passing a monument to Arthur Sullivan to leave the gardens at the far end, just before Waterloo Bridge.

Turn left into Savoy Street where in the shadow of the Savoy Hotel is the historic Queen's Chapel of the Savoy, standing on land given to Count Peter of Savoy by King Henry III in 1246. The chapel is owned by Her Majesty the Queen in her role as the Duke of Lancaster. A window in the chapel commemorates Richard D'Oyly Carte, who founded the Savoy Hotel and Savoy Theatre as well as the D'Oyly Carte Opera Company in order to perform the works of Gilbert and Sullivan.

5 At the top of Savoy Street go right on to the Strand. On the left is the church of St Mary le Strand, designed by James Gibbs. In the 17th century a windmill stood where the church is today, and the first hackney carriage stand was established on this spot in 1634. The foundation stone for the church was laid in February 1715.

Opposite the church is Somerset House. This is the home of The Courtauld Gallery – well worth a visit to see its permanent art collections and changing exhibitions. Parts of the 2008 film *The Duchess* were shot at Somerset House. Edward Seymour (uncle to the young Edward VI and brother to Jane Seymour, third wife of Henry VIII) began building a great mansion here in 1547, demolishing a number of churches in the process.

6 Go right down Surrey Street; at the end climb the steps to a paved area where you can sit above the traffic and enjoy views of the river before going down the steps at the far end and right on Temple Place. A gate on the right leads into Temple Garden where a statue of a little girl commemorates the works of Lady Somerset for the temperance cause, and is inscribed 'I was thirsty and ye gave me drink'.

WALK 1 – Exploring the Embankment

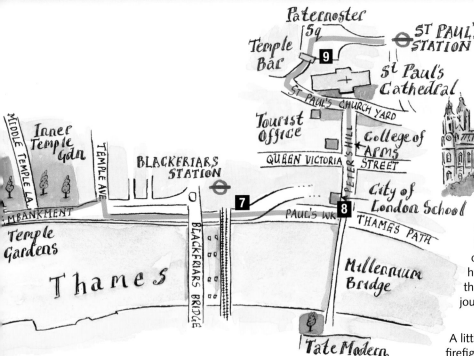

Queen Victoria Street. On your left is the College of Arms, the origins of which lie in the role of medieval heralds whose job it was to record the identifying arms on the shields of jousting knights.

A little further on is a memorial to the firefighters who died defending the nation in the Second World War, inscribed with the words of Winston Churchill who called them 'The heroes with grimy faces'.

Leave the garden here and pass by a pair of dragons – several of which were introduced in the 1960s to mark the boundary of the 'square mile' that is the City of London. Just beyond on the left is a gateway and arched entrance to Middle Temple Lane, leading to Middle and Inner Temples and Temple Church which are explored in Walk 2.

Continue past the railings beyond which lie Inner Temple Gardens and at Temple Avenue cross back to the river and head to Blackfriars Bridge. First built in 1769 it was the third of the London bridges. The structure was replaced 100 years later and renamed for the Black Friars who moved their monastery from Holborn to a site near the bridge in the 13th century.

7 Beside Blackfriars Millennium Pier, go down a slope to Paul's Walk where there are benches to sit and enjoy the view. Along this stretch look for the wall plaque to Baynard's Castle, a stronghold of William the Conqueror which was destroyed in the Great Fire of London in 1666. It was within the castle's walls that Richard, Duke of York was offered the crown – a scene depicted by Shakespeare in *Richard III*.

On the left as you approach Millennium Bridge is a sundial outside the City of London School. The school began with funding from a 15th-century town clerk for the education of four poor boys.

8 Climb the steps up Peter's Hill for a view over the Millennium Bridge to Tate Modern. Turn away from the bridge where ahead of you is the magnificent St Paul's Cathedral. Continue along Peter's Hill, crossing

Around the corner on the left is the City of London Information Centre. Cross here to St Paul's: a cathedral first stood on this site in 604 AD but Sir Christopher Wren's masterpiece has graced London's skyline since 1675. It may not look it from ground level but the ball and cross at the very top of the dome is 23 feet (7 metres) tall – and there is room inside the golden ball for ten people.

9 On the far side of the cathedral go through the archway of Temple Bar into Paternoster Square, a site redeveloped in the early years of the 21st century when the London Stock Exchange relocated here. Pass Paternoster Square column and head right towards the other sculpture in the square, Elisabeth Frink's *Shepherd and Sheep*, reflecting the fact that this was once the site of a livestock market. Continue straight ahead between the shops and buildings beyond the sculpture, finally bearing left to St Paul's Underground station. ●

Millennium Bridge and St Paul's Cathedral

WALK 2 – Capital History and Heritage

DISTANCE: 2½ miles (4 kilometres)
START: St Paul's Underground
END: Chancery Lane Underground

Exit St Paul's Underground following signs for St Paul's Cathedral. Turn left on to Newgate Street, named for one of seven gates in the Roman London Wall. A prison was built at Newgate in 1188, and was the site of public executions from 1783 to 1868 when the last man to be hanged in public in Great Britain met his death here.

1 Cross at the crossing where ahead is Christchurch Greyfriars Garden, on burial ground where a church was first built in the 14th century. The church that stood most recently, designed by Sir Christopher Wren, was destroyed during the Second World War but the rose garden is laid out to match its floor plan, with the box hedge representing the pews.

Cross back over the road, going right on Newgate Street; take the first left opposite Vestry House into Paternoster Square, home to the London Stock Exchange. Gold-leaf flames rise from the top of Paternoster Square column, fashioned from Portland stone. Also in the square is Elisabeth Frink's *Shepherd and Sheep*, a sculpture acknowledging the origins of the area as a livestock market.

St Paul's Cathedral

2 Go through the stone arch which is Temple Bar; it was moved to this spot in 2004 and is the only surviving gate to the City of London. Before you in all its majesty is St Paul's Cathedral, the seat of the Bishop of London. Follow cobbled St Paul's Churchyard round to the right to the main entrance, outside which is a statue of Queen Anne. The cathedral is the fourth on this site built following the destruction of its predecessor in the Great Fire of London in 1666. The tomb of its architect, Sir Christopher Wren, is in the crypt.

Leave the cathedral and go straight ahead along Ludgate Hill, passing the Church of St Martin within Ludgate, with its spire designed by Wren. At Ludgate Circus cross into Fleet Street, named for the River Fleet over which it was built, and until the 1980s the home of British journalism.

Dr Johnson's House

Temple Church

St Paul's Cathedral

WALK 2 – Capital History and Heritage

3 Go straight ahead, taking the second left to St Bride's Avenue and St Bride's Church – another casualty of the Great Fire and rebuilt by Wren. The unusual spire, added in 1701, is known as the 'wedding cake steeple' and is said to be the inspiration for modern-day wedding cakes. In the crypt, along with Roman remains, are displays commemorating the church's long association with the newspaper business.

Back on Fleet Street, on the left is Salisbury Court where a plaque acknowledges the birthplace of diarist Samuel Pepys. Cross Fleet Street, bearing left then right to Wine Office Court and Ye Olde Cheshire Cheese. The building has been a pub since the 16th century but was previously part of a monastery – you can still see parts of the original 13th-century vaults in the cellar. Continue along Wine Office Court and turn left to Gough Square and Dr Johnson's House, where Samuel Johnson worked in the garret to compile the first English Dictionary, published in 1755.

4 With Dr Johnson's House immediately in front of you go left into Johnson's Court, following the pavement to rejoin Fleet Street. Go right to St-Dunstan-in-the-West where a church of the same name has stood since c.1070. Pepys worshipped here and would have seen the two giants turn their heads as they strike the clock on the hour and quarter hour. The clock appears in *Table Talk*, an epic poem by William Cowper:

> … the two figures at St Dunstan's stand,
> Beating alternately, in measured time,
> The clock-work tintinnabulum of rhyme …

5 Just before Chancery Lane cross to the other side of Fleet Street to the black and white timbered Prince Henry's Room, a survivor of the Great Fire of 1666. Built in 1610 as a tavern, The Prince's Arms (later The Fountain), it was frequented by Samuel Pepys who referred to the latter in his diary. There is wonderful carved paneling and stained glass inside and at one time Pepys memorabilia was on display but sadly it is no longer open to the public.

Turn immediately left alongside Prince Henry's Room into Inner Temple Lane leading to Temple Church in the grounds of two of the Inns of Court. The Inns of Court consist of the Inner Temple, Middle Temple, Lincoln's Inn and Gray's Inn. Famous in recent times for its links to Dan Brown's best-seller, *The Da Vinci Code*, in the 12th century the Knights Templar built Temple Church on this site beside the River Thames; it is now the parish church of Inner and Middle Temples. Two hundred years later, the site was offering accommodation and hospitality to law practitioners and students, hence the name 'Inns of Court'. By the late 16th century the Inns had developed into their present form, having the exclusive right to call its members to the Bar and is where barristers and judges spend a large part of their professional lives.

6 Leave Temple Church and head left through the cloisters and down the steps to Fig Tree Court. With Elm Court on your right, turn left at the end of the little garden, passing Lamb Buildings on your right. Go down the steps and through the arch where opposite is the entrance to Inner Temple Garden, a lovely place to sit. Leave the garden, going left on Crown Office Row; head straight on through the arch into Middle Temple Lane and turn right. It was in Middle Temple that William Shakespeare's *Twelfth Night* was first performed in 1602.

7 From Middle Temple Lane rejoin Fleet Street where it meets the Strand. Turn left along the Strand until you come to a statue of Samuel Johnson and the church of St Clement Danes – the central church of the RAF – where amongst other statues is that of Lord Dowding, Commander in Chief of Fighter Command during the Battle of Britain in 1940.

Back on the Strand, cross the road to the Royal Courts of Justice, situated in the middle of the four Inns of Court. This fine Gothic building was opened by Queen Victoria in 1882 and though very much a working court is open for the public to explore the fascinating historical law courts.

8 Leaving the courts, go left along Bell Yard (notice the bell above No. 8, Bell House), turning left into Carey Street and passing the 1603 pub The Seven Stars. Turn right into Serle Street, left into Portugal Street and right into Portsmouth Street where you will find The Old Curiosity Shop. Dating from the mid 16th century, it is thought to be the oldest shop in central London and the inspiration for the novel of the same name by Charles Dickens, who lived in nearby Bloomsbury.

A very fine cat indeed

Opposite Dr Johnson's House in Gough Square is Hodge — 'a very fine cat indeed' — who belonged to Samuel Johnson. Hodge sits on a dictionary and appears to have just devoured an oyster. In the 1791 biography *The Life of Samuel Johnson*, the author James Boswell writes: 'I never shall forget the indulgence with which he treated Hodge, his cat: for whom he himself used to go out and buy oysters.'

From Portsmouth Street you emerge on Lincoln's Inn Fields. Left of the central gardens at No.13 is the Sir John Soane's Museum. Architect Soane negotiated an Act of Parliament, which came into force on his death in 1837, enabling the house and his collections to be preserved for the study of architecture, painting and sculpture. The collection includes such national treasures as William Hogarth's *A Rake's Progress* and the Naseby Jewel, said to have been dropped by Charles I at the battle of Naseby in 1645.

9 With the museum on your left continue along Lincoln's Inn Fields, bearing right along Newman's Row and left through the gate into Lincoln's Inn with its fine buildings rich in tradition. Pass Lincoln's Inn Chapel on your left and carry straight on where in front of you is Old Hall, at one time a dining hall and court room. Go left here to Old Square where high on the wall is the sign: 'The Porters and Police have orders to remove all Persons making a noise within the Inn'. Turn right at Stone Buildings and go through the gateway, turning left on to Chancery Lane.

10 Go right on to High Holborn, immediately left into Fulwood Place and through the narrow gate to Gray's Inn – the fourth and final of the Inns of Court. The gardens here – known as 'the Walks' – were designed by Sir Francis Bacon, treasurer here in the early 17th century. Bear right in front of the gardens through the arch 'To Gray's Inn Square'. Keeping Gray's Inn Chapel on your right, go under the archway straight ahead which brings you out on Gray's Inn Road.

Turn right here, where at the end at the junction with High Holborn is Chancery Lane Underground, opposite one of the few original Tudor buildings left in London. ●

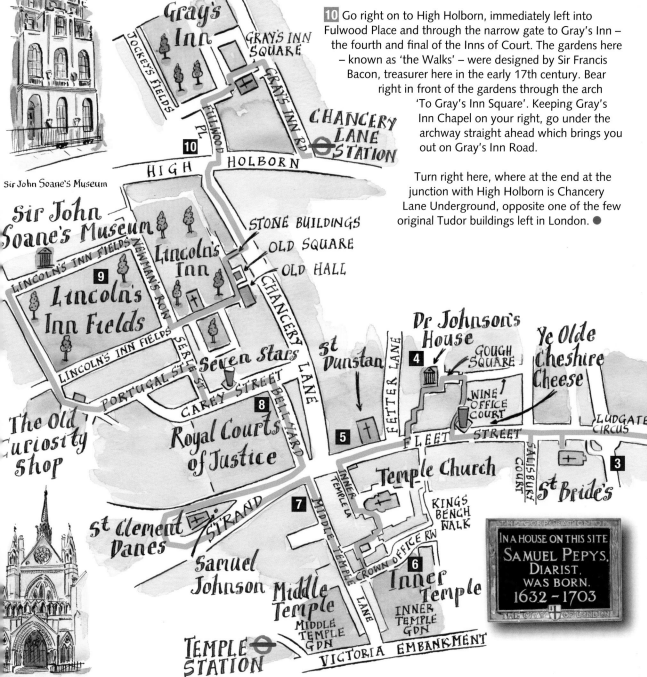

Sir John Soane's Museum

Royal Courts of Justice

WALK 3 – The City's Sights and Delights

DISTANCE: 4 miles (6.5 kilometres)
START: London Bridge Underground
END: Barbican Underground

➤ Leave London Bridge Underground following signs for Tooley Street; to your right is The London Dungeon offering an exciting – if somewhat scary – interactive historical experience deep underground.

1 Turning left out of the station, continue straight ahead and cross the road to Southwark Cathedral. Walk through the cathedral gardens where you can see a sculpture, *The Holy Family,* by Kenneth Hughes. A place of worship has stood here for hundreds of years; the previous church, St Saviours, became Southwark Cathedral in 1905. There is a fascinating history to be explored here, plus a good gift shop and refectory, and visitors are made very welcome.

Leaving the cathedral, follow Montague Close round to London Bridge, beneath which is the entrance to The London Bridge Experience and the London Tombs – more scary entertainment.

2 Go up the steps on to London Bridge, the oldest crossing point over the River Thames and for many years the only entrance to the City. Whilst London is now a much larger metropolis, the term 'The City' relates to approximately one square mile (2.6km^2) that in medieval times would have been the extent of what became the capital of England in the 12th century.

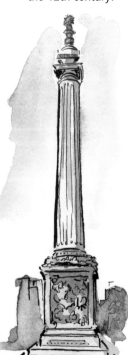

Cross the bridge and continue straight on before turning right into Monument Street where looming before you is The Monument, which you can climb for views over the city. The Monument was created by Sir Christopher Wren in commemoration of the Great Fire of London that started in the early hours of 2 September 1666 in a bakery in Pudding Lane, just 200 feet (60 metres) away.

The Monument

3 Go left up Pudding Lane, then cross Eastcheap, turn left into Philpot Lane and cross to Lime Street, turning left into Leadenhall Market. A market has been on this site since the 1st century AD. Today's restored Victorian covered market featured in the film *Harry Potter and the Philosopher's Stone,* and is a great place to browse the fine produce and stop for refreshments.

The Lloyds Building and the Gherkin

Follow the path through the market and turn right at the Lamb Tavern. Straight ahead you can see the Lloyds Building – a unique structure designed by architect Richard Rogers and opened in 1986. Four successive Lloyds Buildings have been home to the famous ship's bell known as the Lutine Bell since its recovery in 1858. Traditionally rung to inform the brokers when news was received of an overdue ship, today it only tolls when a member of the Royal Family dies, to commemorate Armistice Day and in recognition of disasters such as the London bombings of 7 July 2005.

Turn left as you reach the Lloyds Building and ahead of you is the office block nicknamed the Gherkin; when it opened in 2004 it was the sixth tallest building in London.

4 With the Gherkin on your right and Lloyds on your left go up Leadenhall Street, crossing Bishopsgate to Cornhill where you can see the appropriately named pub The Counting House in the heart of the financial district.

Just past Finch Lane turn right along Royal Exchange Buildings and left to Threadneedle Street, home of the Bank of England. A right turn takes you into Bartholomew Lane and the Bank of England Museum where marvellous collections and changing exhibitions tell the story of the bank and its history dating back to 1694.

Return to Threadneedle Street and continue to the statue of the Duke of Wellington, going past Bank Station and keeping right on to Poultry. Where Threadneedle Street becomes Poultry you will see Mansion House on your left, the official residence of the Lord Mayor of London; this fine example of a Georgian town palace was completed in 1752.

5 Continue along Poultry which becomes Cheapside, then turn left to Bow Churchyard and the church of St Mary le Bow, whose bells have rung in the heart of the City for many centuries. Those born within the sound of the bells are the only people who can claim to be true Cockneys.

7 Turn left along London Wall and cross Wood Street. Next to One London Wall is another section of the historic brickwork and a map showing an outline of the Roman defences. Follow One London Wall as it curves round to the left and take the escalator or lift, following the signs for the Museum of London which is just over the walkway, heralded by Christopher Le Brun's sculpture, *Union – Horse with Discs*. In this remarkable museum you can discover the history of the city from prehistoric times to the present day.

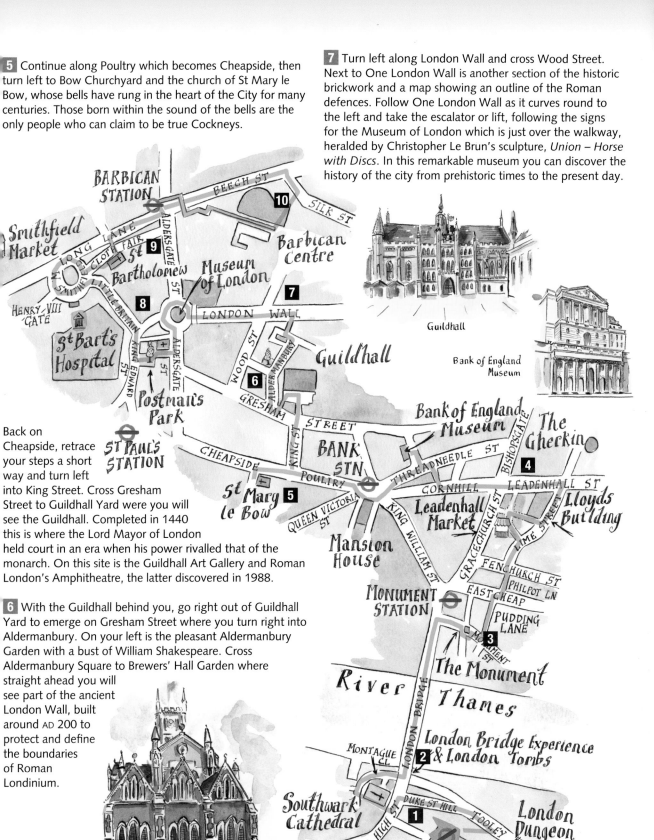

Guildhall

Bank of England Museum

Back on Cheapside, retrace your steps a short way and turn left into King Street. Cross Gresham Street to Guildhall Yard were you will see the Guildhall. Completed in 1440 this is where the Lord Mayor of London held court in an era when his power rivalled that of the monarch. On this site is the Guildhall Art Gallery and Roman London's Amphitheatre, the latter discovered in 1988.

6 With the Guildhall behind you, go right out of Guildhall Yard to emerge on Gresham Street where you turn right into Aldermanbury. On your left is the pleasant Aldermanbury Garden with a bust of William Shakespeare. Cross Aldermanbury Square to Brewers' Hall Garden where straight ahead you will see part of the ancient London Wall, built around AD 200 to protect and define the boundaries of Roman Londinium.

Southwark Cathedral

WALK 3 – The City's Sights and Delights

Leave the museum and go back over the walkway and down to street level. Cross the road and go left on Aldersgate Street where in front of you is the church of St Botolph-without-Aldersgate. Next to it is Postman's Park, named for the postmen who worked in the one-time sorting office in nearby King Edward Street.

8 Exit on the far side of the park and go right on King Edward Street and left into Little Britain where the road leads between the buildings of Britain's oldest hospital, St Bartholomew's, affectionately known as Bart's. Go left at West Smithfield to the Henry VIII gate, an entrance to the hospital through which you go to reach St Bartholomew's Museum where you can trace the history of the hospital from the 12th century.

Keep the Henry VIII gate on your left and follow the road as it bends round to the right (with Haberdasher's Hall on your left) to Smithfield Market. Livestock was sold on this site as early as the 10th century and the market, today housed in a Victorian Grade II listed building, is still particularly famous for its meat, poultry and cheese.

9 With the market on your left, continue on West Smithfield then cross Cloth Fair to the entrance to the church of St Bartholomew the Great. In recent years the oldest parish church in London has appeared in several films including *Four Weddings and a Funeral*. Walk through the churchyard to emerge on Cloth Fair and turn immediately left into Rising Sun Court and right on to Long Lane.

Turn left to Aldersgate Street. On your left is Barbican Underground; go through the entrance and take the stairs immediately on your right to Barbican Highway. Follow the signs to the Barbican Centre; this route brings you to the Lakeside Terrace with fountains and a café. The Barbican was first built by the Romans to protect their new settlement by the river. Over the centuries the area became highly populated, and many residents fell victim to The Great Plague. It became increasingly dilapidated and was laid to waste by bombs during the Second World War. Reconstruction started in 1971 and the complex you see today opened in 1982. It is now Europe's biggest multi-arts centre and here you will find bars, restaurants, bookshops and a range of exhibitions and festivals.

10 Walk through the Barbican Centre building, following signs for Silk Street (the main entrance to the complex). Turn left and left again into Beech Street where you will see the Barbican Underground ahead. ●

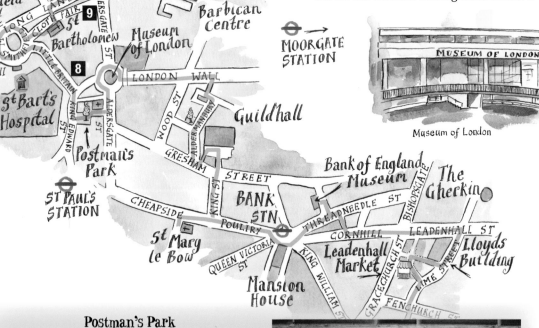

Museum of London

Postman's Park

In Postman's Park is a memorial 'To Heroic Self Sacrifice', devised by Victorian artist George Frederic Watts and unveiled in 1900. It would be difficult not to be moved by the inscriptions on the hand-lettered Royal Doulton tiles honouring ordinary people, many of them children, who lost their lives helping others. There are 47 tablets: the most recent, dated 7 June 2007, commemorates 30-year-old Leigh Pitt who 'saved a drowning boy from the canal at Thamesmead, but sadly was unable to save himself'.

WALK 4 – Literary London

DISTANCE: 3½ miles (5.5 kilometres)
START: Tottenham Court Road Underground
END: Tottenham Court Road Underground

Leave the Underground via the exit signed Tottenham Court Road and New Oxford Street to emerge outside the Dominion Theatre, dating from 1928. The theatre was built on the site of a brewery, where in 1814 a huge porter vat burst; the force of the ensuing flood of beer caused buildings to collapse and eight people died.

1 With the theatre on your right go along Tottenham Court Road where many shops are best known for selling all things electrical. Turn right on to Bayley Street where neat Georgian houses lead to Bedford Square where there are several blue plaques to be seen, including one to Chancellor Lord Eldon, who in 1872 eloped with the love of his life, Bessie Surtees, as both families objected to their relationship. This is the only remaining complete Georgian square in Bloomsbury – an area developed in the 17th century on the estate of the Dukes of Bedford. It was here in 1848 that a group of poets and artists, including Dante Gabriel Rossetti, William Holman Hunt and John Everett Millais, founded the Pre-Raphaelite Brotherhood in protest against sombre Victorian style and values.

2 Leave Bedford Square at the far corner and cross to Montague Place. Go left into Malet Street where you will see the Senate House, home to the library for the University of London. When it was completed in 1937 this 210-feet (64-metre) art deco building was the tallest in London. It is said to have been the inspiration for the Ministry of Truth in George Orwell's book *1984* and also features in John Wyndham's *The Day of the Triffids*; it has appeared in the film versions of both of those books.

Opposite the Senate House, head down Keppel Street and turn right into Gower Street where Charles Darwin lived between 1838 and 1842 and during which time he penned part of *The Origin of Species*. Pass Bonham Carter House on the site where in 1846 the first anaesthetic was administered in England. Shortly after you will pass RADA (the Royal Academy of Dramatic Art), started in 1904 in Haymarket and moving to Gower Street the following year; actors from John Gielgud to Steve McFadden and Glenda Jackson to Jane Horrocks have studied their profession here.

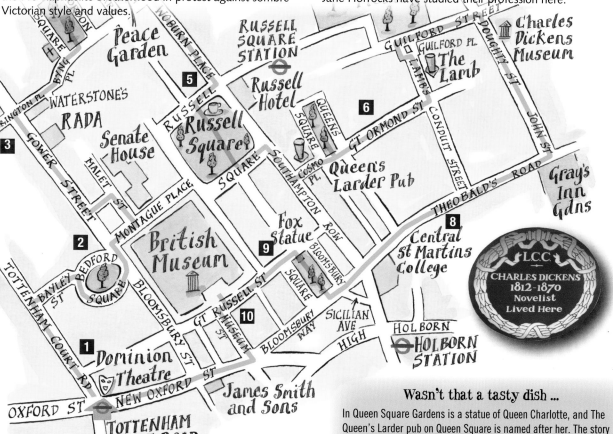

Wasn't that a tasty dish ...

In Queen Square Gardens is a statue of Queen Charlotte, and The Queen's Larder pub on Queen Square is named after her. The story goes that she and her husband, the sickly George III, were residing at his doctor's house on the square while 'Mad King George' received treatment. The queen rented a cellar beneath the pub (then a beer shop) to store and prepare special foods for his health.

WALK 4 –Literary London

3 Turn right on the corner by Waterstone's bookshop (previously Dillons, where regular patron and 20th-century poet Dame Edith Sitwell would give impromptu readings) into Torrington Place, which becomes Byng Place. Go left at the corner to Gordon Square and the English Chapel of Christ the King, built from Bath stone in the mid 1800s. Take the path through Gordon Square Garden to emerge opposite No. 45. Next door at No. 46 lived the Stephen sisters who on marriage became Vanessa Bell and Virginia Woolf. The sisters, along with Virginia's husband, Leonard Woolf, were part of the Bloomsbury Group – a 1920s group of authors and painters whose alternative lifestyle raised many eyebrows.

Go left then right to Endsleigh Place that leads to Tavistock Square. Turn right and go into the 'peace garden'; in its centre is a statue of Mahatma Gandhi, a spiritual and political leader of India who widely advocated non-violence.

Residents of Tavistock Square have included the Woolfs, who moved their increasingly successful Hogarth Press here from Richmond in 1921, publishing works of contemporary fiction, political comment and psychology. Charles Dickens, too, lived here at the old Tavistock House from 1851 to 1860, where he wrote several of his most famous novels including *Bleak House* and *A Tale of Two Cities*.

4 Leave Tavistock Square Garden by the gate opposite Gandhi and go left past the red-brick British Medical Association building on Woburn Place. On the right you will see Woburn Walk, a pleasant place to stop for refreshments and where Irish poet W.B. Yeats lived from 1895 to 1919. Retrace your steps, passing the BMA once more; a plaque on the railings here remembers those killed on the route 30 bus in the London bombings of 7 July 2005.

Russell Square Garden

5 Continue straight on to Russell Square. Opposite the gardens here is the Russell Hotel with its fine Victorian architecture. Dublin-born Oscar Wilde, who moved to London in 1878, spent his last evening in the city at No. 31 Russell Square before departing England's shores for ever. The publishing company Faber & Faber had offices in the square and poet T.S. Eliot once worked for them here as an editor.

Walk through the gardens at the heart of Russell Square – a lovely place to stroll and maybe stop at the café – to the left-hand exit (just right of the statue of the Duke of Bedford). Head down Southampton Row and turn left into Cosmo Place; cross to Queen Square, developed in 1716 and about which Robert Louis Stevenson wrote: 'Queen Square, Bloomsbury is a little enclosure of tall trees and comely brick houses ….'

6 Carry straight on into Great Ormond Street, best known as home to the famous children's hospital. In 1929 *Peter Pan* author J. M. Barrie gave the hospital the copyright of his book and it receives royalties from this literary classic to this day. In 2005 Geraldine McCaughrean was selected from 200 entries in a worldwide search for an author to write the sequel to Barrie's masterpiece; her book is entitled *Peter Pan in Scarlet*.

Turn left on to Lamb's Conduit Street where The Lamb pub is on your right, a meeting place of the Bloomsbury Group. At Guilford Place cross Guilford Street to Coram's Fields which features in Charles Dickens' *Little Dorritt*. Now a playground (and only adults with children can go in), Coram's Fields was once the site of the Foundling Hospital, established in 1730 by Captain Thomas Coram and where unwanted children and orphans lived.

7 Go right along Guilford Street then right into tree-lined Doughty Street. In 1837 Charles Dickens moved to No. 48 following financial success from the serialization of *The Pickwick Papers*; he completed some of his best-loved works here, including *Oliver Twist* and *Nicholas Nickleby*. His house is now the Charles Dickens Museum and has a fascinating collection of manuscripts, rare editions, paintings and furniture.

Continue along Doughty Street to join John Street; at the end cross Theobald's Road and go right. On the left are the peaceful Gray's Inn Gardens in the grounds of the City Law School, part of the famous Inns of Court (see Walk 2). Alumni have included Mahatma Gandhi and Prime Ministers Clement Attlee and Margaret Thatcher.

8 Keep on Theobald's Road passing Central St Martins College of Art & Design where many famous people have studied, including fashion designer Stella McCartney, design-guru Terence Conran and artists Gilbert and George. Go straight over Southampton Row to Vernon Place. To your left is Italian-styled Sicilian Avenue with its shops and pavement cafés. To your right is Bloomsbury Square, one of the first developed on the Bedford estate in the 17th century. Isaac Disraeli lived at No. 6 between 1817 and 1829 and his son, Benjamin, who later became Prime Minister, shared his home here for a short time. Walk through Bloomsbury Square Gardens and leave by the statue of Whig politician Charles James Fox which was erected in 1816, ten years after his death; it portrays him as a Roman holding the Magna Carta, in recognition of his championing of liberty.

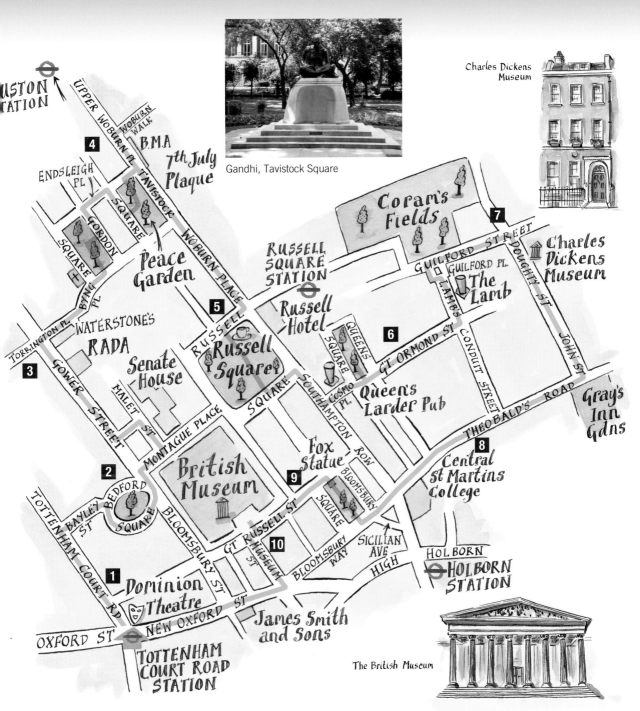

Gandhi, Tavistock Square

Charles Dickens Museum

The British Museum

9 Turn left to Great Russell Street, home to the British Museum with its amazing artefacts of the cultures of the world. The British Museum was first established on this site in a 17th-century mansion, and opened in 1759 with free entry to 'all studious and curious persons'. By the late 19th century the collection was so vast that in 1895 the trustees bought many of the surrounding houses from the Duke of Bedford, which were demolished and enabled the museum to expand. The Reading Room at the heart of the museum took three years to build. When this beautiful domed room – with papier mâché ceiling – opened in 1857, over 60,000 people came to view it at special event over a nine-day period.

10 Go down Museum Street, opposite the British Museum. No. 41 once housed Mandrake Press, who published books for the magician and author Aleister Crowley; No. 49 is home to Atlantis Bookshop, one of London's oldest bookstores and where Crowley spent many hours. Turn right on to New Oxford Street where on your left is the charming Victorian shopfront of James Smith and Sons, Umbrella and Stick Stores, which has been in the same family since it was established in 1830.

Continue along New Oxford Street to return to Tottenham Court Road Underground. ●

WALK 5 – West End Culture and Charm

DISTANCE: 3½ miles (5.5 kilometres)
START: Piccadilly Circus Underground
END: Covent Garden Underground

Leave Piccadilly Circus Underground by exit 4, following the sign to Haymarket and Eros.

As you emerge, immediately ahead of you is the statue known as Eros, the Greek god of love, who stands atop the memorial fountain to Lord Shaftesbury and was unveiled in 1893. Despite popular belief the statue is actually of Eros's brother Anteros, the god of requited or returned love, who better represents philanthropist Shaftesbury's selfless love and good works for the poor. Since 1910 the statue has stood amongst the brightly lit advertising hoardings of Piccadilly, a distinctive feature of this busy junction where several of London's main streets meet.

Eros

Left of Eros is the Criterion Theatre, built on the site of a 17th-century coaching inn. The theatre is underground and during the Second World War was requisitioned by the BBC as a safe place to record and broadcast programmes during the Blitz.

1 With the Criterion Theatre on your right go along Coventry Street; at the corner by the striking *Horses of Helios* statue by Rudy Weller turn right on to Haymarket. As its name suggests, in the 19th century the area was home to a market selling hay. Here you can see the famous Theatre Royal Haymarket where performances have taken place since 1720. Her Majesty's Theatre nearby was named The Queen's Theatre after Queen Anne when it opened in 1705, becoming The King's Theatre in 1714 when George I came to the throne; since then it has changed its name depending who the reigning monarch is.

2 At the end of Haymarket, bear left into Pall Mall. Go left from Pall Mall at the National Gallery Sainsbury Wing into Whitcomb Street. Ahead in the distance you can see the Post Office Tower, built in 1961 and at that time Britain's highest tower.

Cross Coventry Street and continue on Whitcomb Street, turning right into Gerrard Street, the heart of London's Chinatown, where you will find a fantastic choice of oriental restaurants, as well as shops specializing in Chinese foodstuffs. Ronnie Scott's Jazz Club started in the basement of No. 39 Gerrard Street in 1959, moving to nearby Frith Street in 1965, and legend has it that it was also in a Gerrard Street basement that rock group Led Zeppelin held their first rehearsal in 1968.

3 Go left at Gerrard Place and right on to Shaftesbury Avenue, where there is a host of famous London theatres. Along with Piccadilly Circus, Shaftesbury Avenue was built as part of a plan in the late 19th century to link Piccadilly with Bloomsbury, abolishing some of London's worst slums in the process.

From Shaftesbury Avenue, at Cambridge Circus go left along Moor Street which leads to the Prince Edward Theatre, built in 1930 with an art deco foyer and named for the then Prince of Wales, later King Edward VIII.

Go straight along Greek Street which leads to Soho Square, where the garden is a pleasant place to sit. 'So-ho' is said to be a hunting cry and the name dates back to the time when fields here were claimed by Henry VIII as a royal park where he could hunt deer. The area was later developed but by the mid 1800s it had deteriorated and was known for prostitutes and music halls; it retained its poor reputation for much of the 1900s when its pubs become a trendy meeting place for writers, poets and artists. Soho cleaned up its act in the 1980s and is now a multicultural centre for entertainment, as well as being a residential and commercial area.

4 Head out of the garden on to Soho Street and turn right down Oxford Street. Cross at the Dominion Theatre to walk up Tottenham Court Road and take the first right into Great Russell Street.

The British Museum

5 On Great Russell Street is The British Museum which has superb visitor facilities. Opened in 1759 – following a bequest made to King George II by physician, naturalist and collector Sir Hans Sloane – this magnificent collection tells the story of the history of the world's cultures with literally millions of amazing artefacts as diverse as the Rosetta Stone, dating from 196 BC, to a 1947 dinner service and everything imaginable in-between.

Further along Great Russell Street, on the right, is Bloomsbury Square, a fashionable place to live in the 17th century and where Hans Sloane had a medical practice. In the 20th century Bloomsbury became well known as the home of the Bloomsbury Group, artists and writers who originally met at the University of Cambridge and were renowned for their Bohemian way of life.

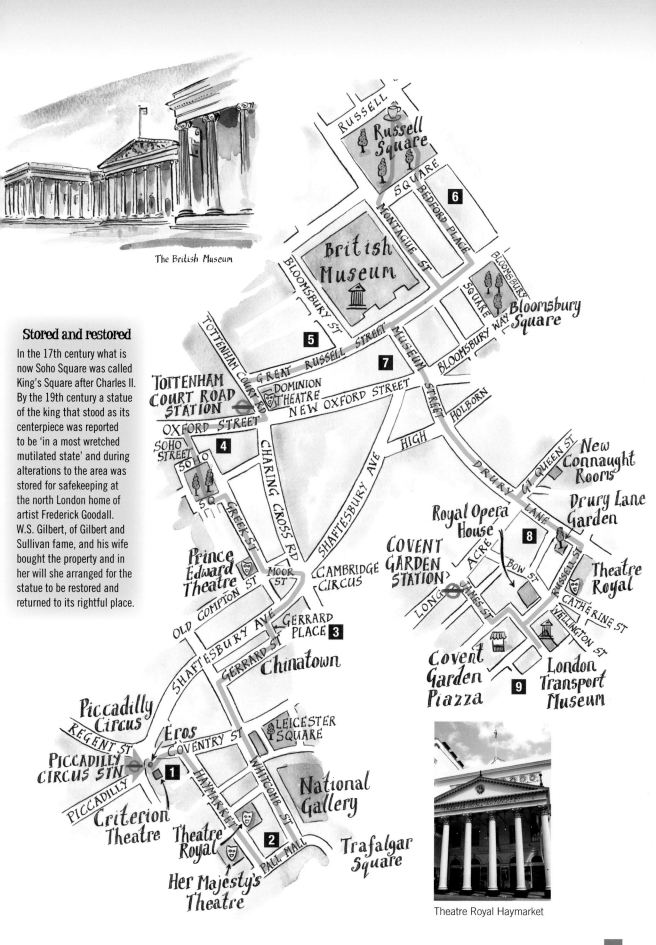

The British Museum

Stored and restored

In the 17th century what is now Soho Square was called King's Square after Charles II. By the 19th century a statue of the king that stood as its centerpiece was reported to be 'in a most wretched mutilated state' and during alterations to the area was stored for safekeeping at the north London home of artist Frederick Goodall. W.S. Gilbert, of Gilbert and Sullivan fame, and his wife bought the property and in her will she arranged for the statue to be restored and returned to its rightful place.

Theatre Royal Haymarket

WALK 5 – West End Culture and Charm

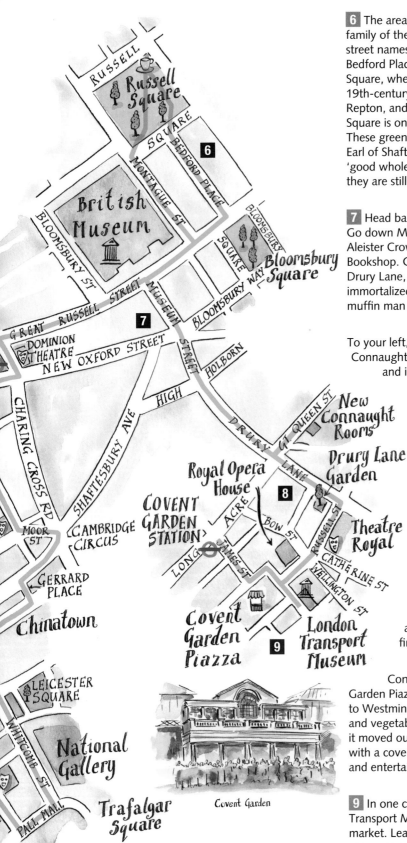

Covent Garden

6 The area is on land linked, through marriage, to the family of the Earls of Bedford since 1669, and many of the street names are a reminder of this. A short walk along Bedford Place, opposite Bloomsbury Square, leads to Russell Square, where the gardens have been styled to the original 19th-century layout by landscape gardener Humphry Repton, and there is a café to enjoy refreshments. At Russell Square is one of London's Grade II listed cabmen's shelters. These green wooden structures were introduced by the Earl of Shaftesbury in the 1870s so that cabmen could enjoy 'good wholesome refreshments at reasonable prices' and they are still used for this purpose today.

7 Head back to the British Museum via Montague Street. Go down Museum Street, opposite the museum, where Aleister Crowley of occult fame frequented the Atlantis Bookshop. Cross New Oxford Street and High Holborn into Drury Lane, another popular area for London theatres, and immortalized in the children's rhyme: 'Do you know the muffin man … who lives in Drury Lane?'

To your left, off Great Queen Street, you can see the New Connaught Rooms. A Masonic hall was built here in 1775, and in 1908 was named the Connaught Rooms after the first Duke of Connaught, Grand Master of the Freemasons. Redeveloped and renamed the New Connaught Rooms in 2006, it is still a venue for prestigious social functions.

8 Continue along Drury Lane, where you will see Drury Lane Garden, another little oasis from the bustle of the city. Go right into Russell Street. On the left is Catherine Street – and the entrance to the famous Theatre Royal Drury Lane which backs on to its namesake. Several theatres have been built on this site, including one designed by Sir Christopher Wren. The current structure, dating from 1812, is the work of Benjamin Wyatt, a young architect who won a competition to rebuild the theatre following a fire three years earlier.

Continue on Russell Street which leads to Covent Garden Piazza. This one-time 'convent garden' belonging to Westminster Abbey evolved to become the largest fruit and vegetable market in England for many centuries, until it moved out in the 1970s. Today the piazza is a lively area with a covered market, outdoor stalls, shops, restaurants and entertainment, and is home to the Royal Opera House.

9 In one corner of Covent Garden Piazza is the London Transport Museum, housed in what was once the flower market. Leave the museum and go straight on keeping the piazza on your left; turn right into James Street where ahead you will see Covent Garden Underground. ●

WALK 6 – Horse Guards and Heroes

DISTANCE: 1 mile (1.5 kilometres)
START: Westminster Underground
END: Leicester Square Underground or Charing Cross Underground

The National Gallery

➤ Exit the Underground following the signs to Westminster Pier and climb the steps on the right to Westminster Bridge. Ahead of you looms the fine sight of Big Ben and the Houses of Parliament.

1 With Big Ben on your left, walk along Bridge Street and go right along Parliament Street, which becomes Whitehall, and past the Cenotaph. The word 'cenotaph' originates from the Greek and means 'empty tomb'. The only words on the structure, commemorating those who lost their lives in the First World War, are Rudyard Kipling's simple phrase: 'The glorious dead.' Each year a service of remembrance is held here at 11am on the Sunday closest to 11 November, Armistice Day, marking the ending of the war on that day in 1918 but also honouring every Commonwealth battle since that time.

Cenotaph

2 Just beyond on your left is Downing Street. No. 10 has been the home and workplace of Britain's Prime Ministers since 1730 when Sir Robert Walpole took up residence. The road has been gated and guarded since 1989.

Passing Downing Street you come to a bronze sculpture, unveiled in 2005, dedicated to the women of the Second World War with its depiction of their uniforms and working clothes hanging on coat pegs.

Cross the road to the Ministry of Defence building where outside are several statues. Perhaps the most instantly recognizable is that of Field Marshal Montgomery, the British Army officer affectionately known as 'Monty' who led Allied forces at the Battle of El Alamein – a major turning point in the Second World War.

THE WOMEN OF WORLD WAR II

Second World War memorial, Whitehall

WALK 6 – Horse Guards and Heroes

On the corner of Horse Guards Avenue is Banqueting House. This is the only remaining part of the Palace of Whitehall where English monarchs resided from 1530 and where Henry VIII died in 1547. With the exception of Banqueting House, the palace was destroyed by fire in 1698. Visitors can tour the building where on 30 January 1649 King Charles I stepped from a window on to the scaffold to be beheaded, with his final words 'I go from a corruptible to an incorruptible Crown, where no disturbance can be'.

3 Cross Whitehall once more where you can see members of the Household Cavalry on duty at Horse Guards between 10am and 4pm. Go through the gate and arch to Horse Guards Parade. Horse Guards was built on the site of the tiltyard of the Palace of Whitehall where Henry VIII enjoyed jousting, a favourite pastimes. The Household Cavalry you see on duty was formed in 1661 on the orders of King Charles II and consists of two regiments – The Life Guards and the Blues and Royals. You may be lucky enough to see the Changing of the Queen's Life Guard that takes place daily on Horse Guards Parade at 11am (10am on Sundays).

On Horse Guards Parade is the entrance to the Household Cavalry Museum where you can discover the history of the Household Cavalry and enjoy a behind-the-scenes tour to see the 18th-century working stables.

Return to Whitehall and continue left; on the right you will see Great Scotland Yard. This little road backed on to the original Metropolitan Police Commissioner's office at No. 4 Whitehall Place, which accounts for subsequent sites of the Metropolitan Police headquarters being named New Scotland Yard.

Continue along Whitehall and as you approach the junction with Trafalgar Square ahead of you, go left to see Admiralty Arch and a fine view along The Mall to Buckingham Palace. Admiralty Arch adjoins the Old Admiralty Building, and was commissioned by Edward VII in memory of his mother; its Latin inscription translates as 'In the tenth year of King Edward VII, to Queen Victoria, from most grateful citizens, 1910'.

National Portrait Gallery

St Martin-in-the-Fields

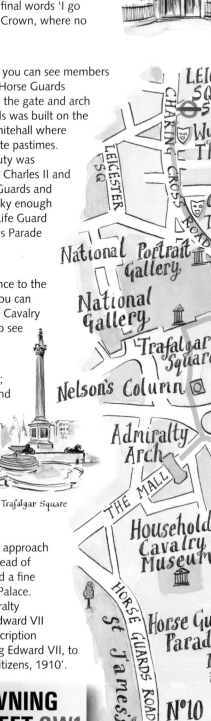

Trafalgar Square

DOWNING STREET SW1
CITY OF WESTMINSTER

Whose nose?

Under the right-hand arch of Admiralty Arch, as you look along The Mall, look hard enough and on the left you will see a 'nose' protruding from the wall. It is about waist height for those passing through on horseback and mounted soldiers would rub it for luck. Some legends say it is the nose of the Duke of Wellington, others that of Edward VII, with claims that each had a large nose. Whose nose? Who knows.

4 Cross to Trafalgar Square and the landmark that is Nelson's Column. The area on which Trafalgar Square stands was at one time the courtyard of the Great Mews, stabling for the Palace of Whitehall. In 1812 the architect John Nash was commissioned to develop the area and he planned 'a new street … forming an open square in the Kings Mews opposite Charing Cross' as a public open space. It opened in 1830 as Trafalgar Square, its name commemorating Britain's naval victory in 1805 during the Napoleonic Wars. Nelson's Column was erected 13 years later.

What is known as the Fourth Plinth was built in 1841 for an equestrian sculpture that never materialized. In recent years it has served as the location for a variety of artworks – perhaps most unusually in 2009 when sculptor Antony Gormley arranged for individuals to occupy the plinth for one hour each, around the clock for 100 days between July and October. The 'plinthers' chose what they wanted to do for their allocated hour: variations included playing the bagpipes in celebration of Robert Burns' 250th anniversary and reading out the names of those in the RAF who died in both world wars on a particular day.

Head between the fountains on Trafalgar Square to The National Gallery, home of the national collection of some of the finest Western European paintings from the 13th to the 19th centuries, including such well-knowns as Vincent van Gogh's *Sunflowers* and John Constable's *The Hay Wain*. Round the corner to the right of The National Galley is the National Portrait Gallery. The gallery holds the most extensive collection of portraits in the world, and also a diverse choice of changing exhibitions. Permanent exhibits include the William Shakespeare portrait attributed to John Taylor and the only one of the great man likely to have been painted from life.

5 Opposite the National Portrait Gallery is the church of St Martin-in-the-Fields. The first reference to a church on this site dates from 1222 though the present building, designed by James Gibbs, was completed in 1726. Very much a living church, alongside its services today St Martin's is a popular venue for classical and jazz concerts. Visitors can enjoy tours, participate in brass rubbing, see exhibitions and enjoy refreshments in the café in the crypt.

To get to Leicester Square Underground, go right out of the church and take the left-hand fork into Charing Cross Road. Continue past the Garrick Theatre on your right. Opened in 1889, and funded by W.S. Gilbert of Gilbert and Sullivan fame, it is named after 18th-century actor David Garrick.

Shortly after you come to Wyndham's Theatre where, after success on Broadway, *Godspell* opened in 1972 with a cast including David Essex and Jeremy Irons. Madonna made her West End debut here in 2002 in *Up For Grabs*. Leicester Square Underground is next to the theatre.

Alternatively, to get to Charing Cross Underground, go left out of St Martin's to Duncannon Street where the station is ahead of you. ●

Trafalgar Square, The National Gallery and St Martin-in-the-Fields

WALK 7 – Royal Palaces, Parks and Pageantry

DISTANCE: 4 miles (6.5 kilometres)
START: Victoria Underground
END: St James's Park Underground

Exit Victoria Station following the signs for Buckingham Palace to emerge on Victoria Street. Go right along here, passing the Victoria Palace Theatre on your left and Little Ben on your right, a small replica of the famous Big Ben clock tower.

1 Continue on Victoria Street until on the right you come to Westminster Cathedral, the Mother Church of Roman Catholicism in England and Wales. It has a magnificent interior and you can go up the tower for 360 degree views over London.

Leave the cathedral and cross Victoria Street to walk through Cardinal Walk, the glass-covered shopping area opposite. Pass the green glass sculpture and turn left past the escalator. Bear right on to Bressenden Place, following signs for Buckingham Place.

2 Go right into Buckingham Palace Road to the Royal Mews, which are working stables and also house the state carriages and motor cars used by the Royal Family.

Continue along Buckingham Gate; on your left is The Queen's Gallery, created in what was once a chapel, heavily damaged by wartime bombing. The gallery houses impressive exhibitions of many types of art and treasures belonging to the Royal Collection – from paintings and jewellery to books and armour.

Just beyond is the grand gated entrance to Buckingham Palace. The State Rooms are open to the public for a few weeks each summer. As well as being the official London residence of the reigning monarch since Queen Victoria's time, it is also Her Majesty Queen Elizabeth II's administrative headquarters, and where she entertains heads of state. The original Buckingham House was built for the Duke of Buckingham in 1703, eventually being redeveloped into a grander affair about which Queen Victoria said 'I delight in Buckingham Palace'; she took up residence just three weeks after ascending the throne.

3 Opposite Buckingham Palace is the imposing Victoria Memorial, where the marble queen looks towards The Mall. Facing Queen Victoria, and with your back to The Mall, cross the road to the right and enter Green Park alongside the ornate Canada Gate. Just beyond is the Canada Memorial, an unusual fountain decorated with maple leaves in memory of the Canadian soldiers from the First and Second World Wars.

Go along Constitution Hill, which is so named because Charles II, who claimed what was meadowland as a royal park, took his daily walk (or constitutional) here. At the top of Constitution Hill are the Memorial Gates honouring the volunteers from the Indian subcontinent, Africa and the Caribbean who served alongside the British Armed Forces during both world wars.

4 Turn back into Green Park, taking the path on the diagonal. Go straight on at the Constance Fountain to pass the blue and gold Devonshire gates. These gates were designed by Inigo Jones and at one time were the entrance to Devonshire House, the London mansion of the Dukes of Devonshire that stood on Piccadilly.

5 Follow the path around the edge of the park where it joins Queen's Walk, built for Caroline, queen of George II, in the 18th century. Continue along Queen's Walk (with the park on your right) passing Spencer House (built for the first Earl Spencer) and Lancaster House (originally York House – it changed its name when it was purchased by Lancastrian Lord Leverhulme) which is used for government hospitality. Look for the sign for the charmingly named Milkmaids Passage, along which milk was at one time carried to St James's Palace.

6 Go left out of the park on to The Mall, passing sentries guarding Clarence House and St James's Palace. Clarence House was home to Queen Elizabeth the Queen Mother from 1953 until her death in 2002, when it became the official residence of Prince Charles. It is open to the public for a few weeks each year.

They're changing guard ...

Changing the Guard at Buckingham Palace takes place at 11am, but only on alternate days during certain months. This ancient tradition is a splendid sight to behold, though brought down to earth a little in the A.A. Milne poem 'Buckingham Palace' in which Christopher Robin goes to watch the ceremony with Alice, who is to marry one of the guards:

We saw a guard in a sentry-box.
'One of the sergeants looks after their socks,' says Alice.

Buckingham Palace

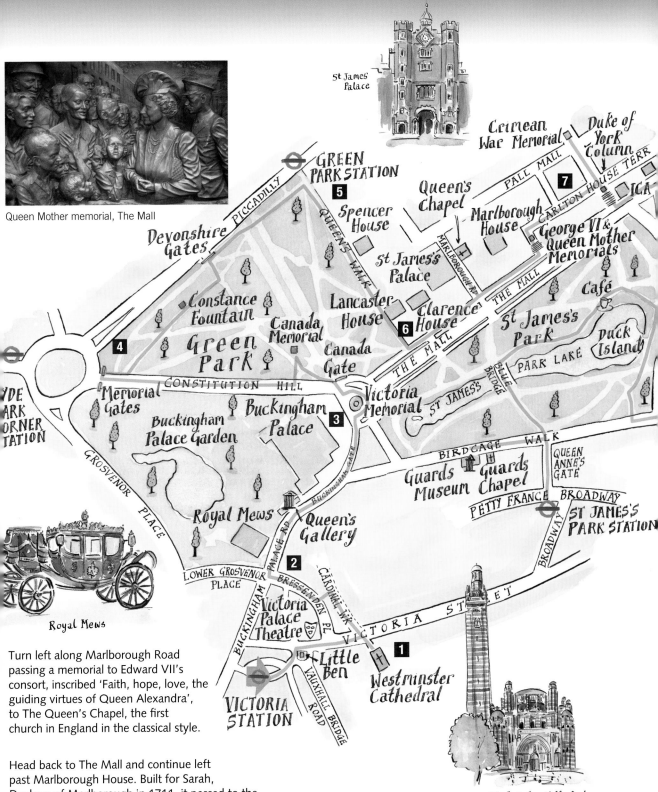

Queen Mother memorial, The Mall

St James' Palace

Crimean War Memorial

Duke of York Column

ICA

7

Pall Mall

Carlton House Terr

GREEN PARK STATION

5

Queen's Chapel

Marlborough House

George VI & Queen Mother Memorials

Piccadilly

Devonshire Gates

Spencer House

The Mall

St James's Park

Café

Queen's Walk

Constance Fountain

Lancaster House

Clarence House

6

Park Lake

Duck Island

Green Park

Canada Memorial

St James's Palace

St James's Park

Blue Bridge

Memorial Gates

Constitution Hill

Canada Gate

Victoria Memorial

St James's

4

Buckingham Palace Garden

Buckingham Palace

3

Birdcage Walk

Queen Anne's Gate

HYDE PARK CORNER STATION

Grosvenor Place

Guards Museum

Guards Chapel

Petty France

Broadway

St James's Park Station

Royal Mews

Queen's Gallery

Broadway

Royal Mews

Lower Grosvenor Place

2

Buckingham Palace Rd

Bressenden Pl

Cardinal Wk

Victoria Street

Victoria Palace Theatre

Little Ben

1

Westminster Cathedral

Victoria Station

Vauxhall Bridge Road

Westminster Cathedral

Turn left along Marlborough Road passing a memorial to Edward VII's consort, inscribed 'Faith, hope, love, the guiding virtues of Queen Alexandra', to The Queen's Chapel, the first church in England in the classical style.

Head back to The Mall and continue left past Marlborough House. Built for Sarah, Duchess of Marlborough in 1711, it passed to the Crown a century later. In 1953 it was donated for use as a Commonwealth research and conference centre. Just beyond Marlborough House are memorials to George VI and his queen. Embossed bronze reliefs show scenes of the Queen Mother during the Second World War and also depict her love of her family, horse racing and dogs.

7 Climb the steps here to Carlton Gardens – where from 1914–15 Earl Kitchener lived at No. 2 – then go right along Carlton House Terrace to Waterloo Place. On the right is the imposing Duke of York Column and on the left more statues lead to Pall Mall and a memorial to the Crimean War, cast in bronze from cannons captured at the siege of Sebastopol.

WALK 7 – Royal Palaces, Parks and Pageantry

Return to the Duke of York Column, dating from 1834. The duke in question is Prince Frederick, son of George III, and the one to whom the children's nursery rhyme is generally attributed. Go down the steps back to The Mall and left to two art centres: the Institute of Contemporary Art and the Mall Galleries.

8 Do a U-turn at Admiralty Arch; pass Captain Cook and go left past the National Police Memorial. Continue left into Horse Guards Road to Horse Guards Parade and the Household Cavalry Museum. Changing the Guard takes place daily at 11am (10am on Sundays) on Horse Guards Parade.

Continue on Horse Guards Road to the Bali memorial, a marble sphere featuring 202 doves representing the number of victims who died in a terrorist attack in Bali in 2002.

9 Just beyond is the entrance to the Churchill Museum and Cabinet War Rooms. The underground tunnels and shelters were constructed between Parliament and Downing Street as a central shelter for government and military strategists during the Second World War. Many of the fascinating exhibits are exactly as they were left when the rooms were closed on 16 August 1945, the day after VJ Day.

At the end of Horse Guards Road go right into Birdcage Walk, taking its name from the aviary of exotic birds James I kept here. Enter St James's Park on the right. With the lake ahead go right and circle the lake with its resident pelicans, passing Duck Island, the Swire fountain and the café. At one time the park was the site of a leper hospital and later a deer park for Henry VIII before James I landscaped it and kept a menagerie of animals on site, including camels and crocodiles. Charles II redesigned the park, opening it to the public and entertaining guests, including his mistress Nell Gwyn.

10 Go left over the Blue Bridge and carry straight on, leaving the park opposite a tall iron gateway (leading to Queen Anne's Gate). Turn right in front of the gateway and go along Birdcage Walk to the Guards Chapel, Guards Museum and The Toy Soldier Centre and Shop. The collection at the Guards Museum relates to the five regiments of Foot Guards: Grenadier, Coldstream, Scots, Irish and Welsh. The Guards Chapel is a peaceful place to visit, but in 1944, during morning service, the chapel was hit by a flying bomb killing 121 soldiers and civilians. Although the building was almost destroyed, amazingly the silver candlesticks and cross remained unmoved, and the candles still burned. The rebuilt chapel opened in 1963.

11 Leave the museum and chapel and go right up Birdcage Walk to return to the iron gateway where you turn right into Queen Anne's Gate; cross Broadway and Petty France to St James's Park Underground. ●

View from the Blue Bridge, St James's Park

WALK 8 – West End Shoppers' Paradise

DISTANCE: 3 miles (5 kilometres)
START: Marble Arch Underground
END: Oxford Circus Underground

Take the Hyde Park exit from Marble Arch Underground where Marble Arch looms on your right.

1 Before venturing to the shops, turn left out of the station and over the crossing to Hyde Park and Speakers Corner – a well-known spot for public speakers to air their views since the 19th century. Anyone can take to their soapbox here, if they can take the heckling; famous orators in the past have included Karl Marx, William Morris and George Orwell.

Continue on Oxford Street and turn right on to South Molton Street for fashionable shops and cafés. Go left at Brook Street and right into New Bond Street to continue the exclusive fashion shopping experience.

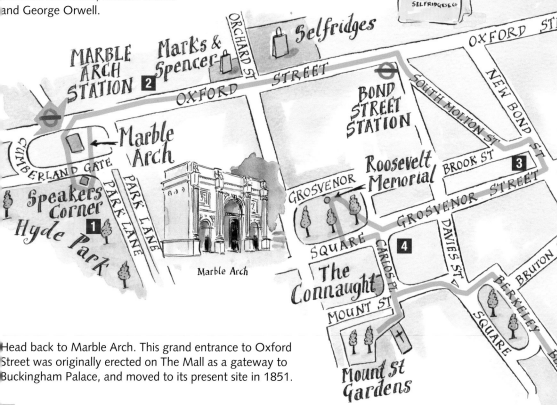

Marble Arch

Head back to Marble Arch. This grand entrance to Oxford Street was originally erected on The Mall as a gateway to Buckingham Palace, and moved to its present site in 1851.

2 Turn right into Oxford Street with its vast choice of shops to suit all pockets. One of the first major stores on the left is Marks and Spencer – this flagship store opened in 1930 on the site of what was once a Victorian department store, Pantheon Bazaar. As one Victorian author wrote: 'And so into the Pantheon, turning and turning about in that Hampton Court-like maze of stalls, laden with pretty gimcracks … .'

Opposite M&S, and at the junction with Orchard Street, is Selfridges. The store was founded in 1909 by American Henry Gordon Selfridge, thought to have invented the phrase 'the customer is always right'. It is well worth stepping inside to experience this wonderful piece of history and imagine the excitement that must have been generated in the store when here in 1925 John Logie Bard demonstrated television in public for the first time.

3 Turn right on to Grosvenor Street, the latter part of which has fine colonnaded Georgian buildings. Outside No. 34 are iron snuffers that in days gone by would have extinguished flamed torches used to light the way on dark nights.

Cross into Grosvenor Square, developed in the 1720s as the centrepiece of the Grosvenor Estate, owned by the Dukes of Westminster, and becoming a public space in 1946. The American Embassy was established at No. 1 Grosvenor Square in 1938, and the statue of Franklin D. Roosevelt added ten years later. A more recent addition to this green area is the memorial garden with its poignant inscription, 'Grief is the price we pay for love' – a tribute to those who lost their lives in the 9/11 tragedy of 2001.

WALK 8 – West End Shoppers' Paradise

Flame snuffer,
Grosvenor Street

4 Leave Grosvenor Square and, back on Grosvenor Street, head across the road to Carlos Place. At the far end is the luxurious Connaught Hotel, built in 1897 and named The Coburg Hotel after Prince Albert of Saxe-Coburg, whose widow was Queen Victoria. Twenty years later it was renamed the Connaught after the royal couple's son, Prince Arthur, Duke of Connaught.

Follow the left-hand side of Berkeley Square which joins Berkeley Street. At the end cross to one of London's most prestigious hotels, The Ritz, opened by hotelier Cesar Ritz in 1906 and where (pre-booked) afternoon tea in the Palm Court is a wonderful treat.

Carnaby Street

Cross into Mount Street Gardens where there are lots of benches to sit and enjoy the tranquillity. Here you will see The Church of the Immaculate Conception, a Jesuit church in the heart of the parish of Mayfair.

Leave by the same gate and go right along Mount Street, bearing right to Berkeley Square where the plane trees are some of the oldest in the capital. Sadly, with the busy traffic, there is little chance of ever hearing a nightingale sing here despite the sentiment expressed in the romantic song of the 1940s, 'A Nightingale Sang in Berkeley Square', popular with many vocalists as diverse as Vera Lynn and Rod Stewart.

Fortnum & Mason

5 Facing The Ritz go left passing pretty Piccadilly Arcade to arrive at Fortnum and Mason, where all sorts of delicious foodstuffs have been sold on Piccadilly for over 300 years. Its origins lie with shopkeeper Hugh Mason who let a room to William Fortnum, a footman to the Royal Family who was able to acquire unused wax from the royal candles, the profits of which enabled them to start a business.

Next door to Fortnum and Mason is the oldest surviving bookshop in London, Hatchards, founded in 1797 and now part of Waterstone's.

Continue on Piccadilly and go right along Princes Arcade, with its charming array of old-fashioned shop fronts, to Jermyn Street where you turn left. Jermyn Street, dating back to 1664 and named for Henry Jermyn, the Earl of St Albans, is synonymous with men's high-quality shirts. Today it is also a great place to go for a wide range of other goods, and it is here that you can visit Paxton and Whitfield, cheesemongers since 1797, who stock a magnificent range of cheeses and other fine foods.

6 Turn left alongside St James's Church (designed by Christopher Wren and said to be his favourite) and left again to rejoin Piccadilly where on certain days a market takes place in the courtyard of the church.

Cross the road and continue left, looking up to spot the inscription above a building to your left: 'Royal Institute of Painters in Watercolours 1831'; in a few steps you come to Burlington House, home to the Royal Academy of Arts which has changing exhibitions and events. Dating from 1664, Burlington House is the only surviving mansion on Piccadilly. Enter its magnificent gateway where in the courtyard stands a statue of Sir Joshua Reynolds, one of the founding members of the academy.

Hamleys

Next door to Burlington House is Burlington Arcade with a fine range of quality shops. At the far end of Burlington Arcade turn right on to Burlington Gardens and left into Savile Row, world renowned for bespoke men's tailoring and still home to such famous names as Hardy Amies and Ozwald Boateng. In the late 1960s, No. 3 Savile Row was the headquarters of Apple Corps Ltd, founded by The Beatles who recorded under the Apple label.

7 Turn right at New Burlington Street and left into Regent Street. A short way along on the right is Hamleys – seven floors of fun for children of all ages with every imaginable toy and game.

Just beyond Hamleys turn right along Foubert's Place which leads to Carnaby Street. Famous in the 1960s for its boutiques, there are still lots of fashion shops here, many of them independent labels.

Liberty

8 Go left along Carnaby Street and left again at the end into Great Marlborough Street where you will find another famous London store – Liberty, whose Tudor-style building actually dates from the 1920s, and was constructed with timbers from two ships. This beautiful emporium was started in the late 19th century by Arthur Lasenby Liberty, a champion of the designs of the Arts and Craft and Art Nouveau movements.

Opposite Liberty is Argyll Street, home of the London Palladium. A theatre opened here in 1910 but before that the venue had been a circus and an ice-skating rink. The London Palladium is renowned for its variety shows and hosted the first Royal Variety Performance in 1930. It was here in 1963 that The Beatles first performed in a nationally broadcast show.

9 From Great Marlborough Street turn right into Regent Street and continue straight ahead for Oxford Circus and the Underground. ●

WALK 9 – Kensington Palace and Gardens

DISTANCE: 2½ miles (4 kilometres)
START: Lancaster Gate Underground
END: Queensway Underground

 Leave Lancaster Gate Station following signs to Bayswater Road.

1 Cross Bayswater Road and go through Marlborough Gate into Kensington Gardens. Once part of Hyde Park, the land was purchased in 1689 by William III (William of Orange) who found the air and quiet location agreeable for his asthma. It was not until the 18th century that the gardens were opened, on Saturdays, to the public – and only then to the 'respectably dressed'.

Kensington Palace

Ahead of you are the Italian Gardens, commissioned by Queen Victoria in 1860. They appear in a scene in the film *Bridget Jones: The Edge of Reason* when the characters played by Hugh Grant and Colin Firth have a water fight here.

With the fountains on your left, follow The Long Water, par of The Serpentine, created in 1728 by Queen Caroline, wife of George II.

2 Shortly you come to the Peter Pan statue. This enchanting sculpture was commissioned by *Peter Pan* author J.M. Barrie and placed here during the night so that on May Day 1912 children seeing it might think the fairies had brought it. Part of the 2004 film about Barrie, *Finding Neverland* (with Johnny Depp playing Barrie), was shot in these gardens where the author met the family of boys who are said to have inspired the character Peter Pan. Just beyond Peter Pan the path forks; take the right-hand path to the Serpentine Gallery with its collection of modern and contemporary art.

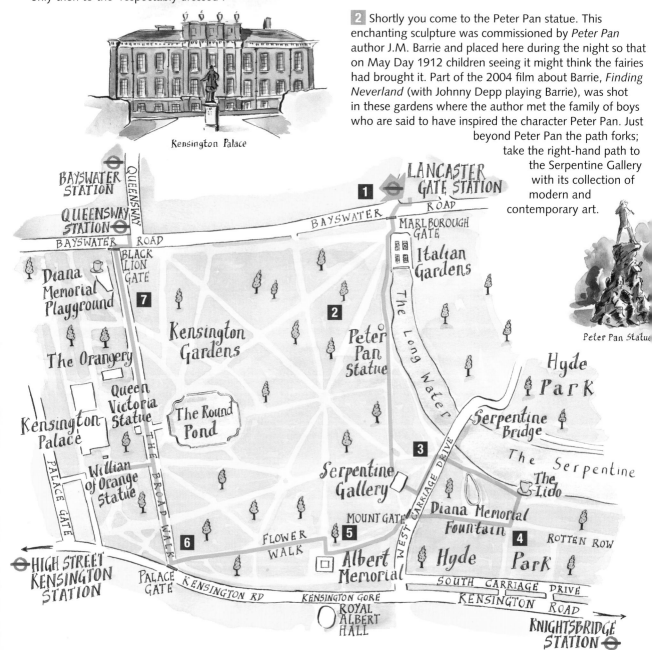

Peter Pan Statue

3 Leave the gallery and head towards the Serpentine Bridge, dating from the 1820s and marking the boundary between Kensington Gardens and Hyde Park. Cross the road into Hyde Park; on the right is the Diana Memorial Fountain, where on a hot day you are likely to find lots of people enjoying keeping cool.

4 Turn right along the path that runs between the fountain and The Lido café. Turn right again and follow the path, crossing West Carriage Drive to re-enter Kensington Gardens at Mount Gate.

William of Orange statue

5 Keep left here and head for the Albert Memorial, a glorious monument to the consort of Queen Victoria who died aged 42. The memorial is a celebration of his love of the arts and his contribution to Victorian society represented in carvings including manufacture, commerce, agriculture and engineering. The pathway behind the memorial takes you through Flower Walk where there are many opportunities to sit and enjoy the gardens.

6 At Palace Gate go right on to The Broad Walk, following signs for the Round Pond and Queensway. Where the paths cross, the left-hand path takes you to Kensington Palace South Garden where there is a statue of William III.

Albert Memorial

Return to The Broad Walk where on your left is a statue of Queen Victoria by one of her daughters, Princess Louise; on your right is the Round Pond introduced by Queen Caroline at the same time as she created The Serpentine. The pond was designed so that avenues of trees surrounding the water led to different views of the palace.

A few steps past the statue of Queen Victoria is the main entrance to Kensington Palace, originally Nottingham House before it was purchased and renamed by King William and Queen Mary following renovations by Sir Christopher Wren. It became a principal royal residence for several subsequent monarchs. Queen Victoria was born at Kensington and it was here in 1837 that the 18-year-old princess learned of her accession to the throne on the death of her uncle, William IV. The young queen, however, chose to make Buckingham Palace her home, after which Kensington Palace fell into disrepair. It was eventually saved by funding from Parliament and the newly restored State Apartments opened to the public on Queen Victoria's 80th birthday, 24 May 1899.

In more recent times one of the apartments in Kensington Palace was the home of Diana, Princess of Wales. She lived here following her marriage to Prince Charles in 1981 until her death on 31 August 1997 when millions of flowers were laid at the palace gates in a national outpouring of grief. It was from here that her funeral procession started on its journey to Westminster Abbey.

7 Continue on The Broad Walk: the Diana Princess of Wales Memorial Playground on the left is a good spot for children to burn off any surplus energy, and there is a café here too.

Leave the gardens just beyond the café, at Black Lion Gate. Cross Bayswater Road and go right then left into Queensway and the Underground. ●

Tea at the palace

We have Queen Anne to thank for The Orangery, just past the main entrance to Kensington Palace and a delightful spot to enjoy refreshments, including delicious traditional afternoon tea.

Queen Anne moved to Kensington when she ascended the throne in 1702 on the death of her sister, Queen Mary. Queen Anne took a keen interest in developing the gardens and spent £26,000 (the equivalent of over £2 million today) improving them. The Orangery was built to house citrus trees and other exotic plants during the winter months, but the sumptuous interior also made it suitable for entertaining.

DISTANCE: 3½ miles (5.5 kilometres)
START: Knightsbridge Underground
END: Hyde Park Corner Underground

Leave Knightsbridge Underground following signs for Brompton Road.

1 Go left on to Brompton Road to see the fabulous window displays enticing you into Harrods. Harrods' modest origins lie with 1930s East End grocer and tea merchant Charles Henry Harrod, from which grew 'the world's most famous department store'. Travelling the magnificent escalator flanked by the story of Ancient Egypt as you glide up seven floors, one can only imagine the scene in 1898 when the first 'moving staircase' in the world was installed here, an experience which led to customers being revived with brandy on reaching the top. If you don't have time to explore the maze of departments in the whole store, the food hall on the ground floor is a must, being architecturally beautiful (as well as mouth-watering).

2 Continue on Brompton Road and at the junction keep right on to Thurloe Place where on the right are Holy Trinity Brompton – one of London's most popular churches – and the domed Oratory of St Philip Neri. This is the second largest Catholic church in London and was built in the latter half of the 19th century when the area was still fields and lanes.

Stay on Thurloe Place to the Victoria & Albert Museum where you can roam at will or enjoy a free guided tour that introduces you to the museum's history and its amazing, diverse range of artefacts, dating from centuries BC to modern day.

Opposite the entrance to the V&A, a blue plaque at No. 33 Thurloe Square marks the one-time home of Sir Henry Cole. As well as being the first director of the V&A, along with Queen Victoria's consort Prince Albert he was involved with the Great Exhibition of 1851, dedicated to commerce and industry, the success of which led to the founding of the V&A Museum, the Natural History Museum and the Science Museum.

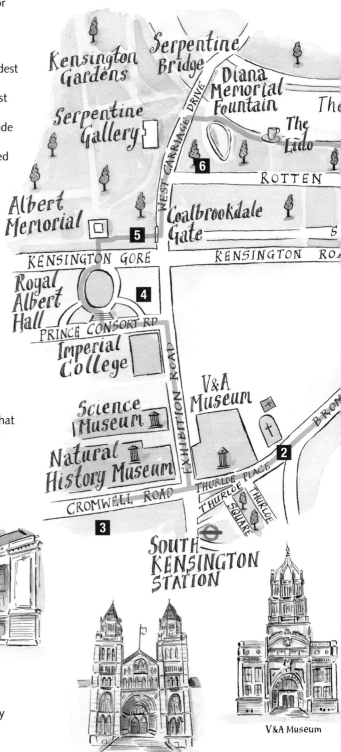

Science Museum

Natural History Museum

V&A Museum

Also opposite the V&A is a small park with a sculpture by Angela Conner entitled *Twelve Responses to Tragedy*; it recalls the Soviet citizens who attended a conference regarding repatriation at Yalta in 1943 and were killed on their return to the USSR.

King's Hunting Ground

3 From Thurloe Place cross Exhibition Road to Cromwell Road and the entrance to the Natural History Museum. The museum has been on this site since 1881 and proudly claims its status as the largest and most important natural history collection in the world. Facilities include the state-of-the-art Darwin Centre where visitors can experience science in action.

Leaving the museum go left on Cromwell Road and left again on Exhibition Road to the Science Museum. Here are collections, galleries and exhibitions loved by all ages and you can see everything from *Puffing Billy*, the oldest surviving steam train, to a film in the 3-D IMAX cinema. There are lots of hands-on opportunities too.

Harrods' food hall

Continue along Exhibition Road past Imperial College with striking award-winning architecture by Sir Norman Foster.

4 Turn left into Prince Consort Road where you will find the Royal Albert Hall on the right and can enjoy a pre-arranged tour. The design of the building takes its inspiration from Roman amphitheatres and was completed in 1871 in memory of Prince Albert. Exhibitions and ceremonies take place here but the Albert Hall is best known for its concerts: Elgar, Verdi and Wagner all conducted the first performances of their own works in the UK here, and other musical artistes have included everyone from Frank Sinatra to The Beatles to Kaiser Chiefs.

On the far side of the Albert Hall cross Kensington Gore to Kensington Gardens and the Albert Memorial, commissioned by Queen Victoria on her husband's death in 1861. There can be few grander memorials, and the design celebrates the prince's interests, with figures at each corner representing Africa, America, Asia and Europe, and, higher up, those to agriculture, commerce, engineering and manufacture – all topped by gilded angels of virtue.

5 Facing the Albert Memorial, go right along the path and through Coalbrookdale Gate. Turn left along West Carriage Drive, passing sand-covered Rotten Row, a bridleway dating from 1690. Rotten Row was created by William III to link Kensington Palace with Westminster and was the first lamp-lit roadway in the country. Its name is likely to be from the French *route de roi* (King's Road).

Opposite the Serpentine Gallery, and just before Serpentine Bridge, turn right into Hyde Park which stretches for 350 acres (140 hectares). The park is named for the manor of Hyde which belonged to the monks of the Abbey of Westminster. At the Dissolution of the Monasteries in 1536 the area was was acquired by Henry VIII as a hunting ground, and limited access was only granted to the public by James I in the early 17th century.

6 On the right you will see the Diana Memorial Fountain, designed by Kathryn Gustafson for everyone to get in and have fun, reflecting the princess's inclusive personality and love of children.

Walk through the park alongside the lake – The Serpentine, created in the 18th century by Queen Caroline, wife of George II, and on the shores of which was built the Crystal Palace that housed Prince Albert's Great Exhibition. The great glass building was designed by Joseph Paxton. The architect's previous occupation as head gardener at Chatsworth (the Derbyshire country seat of the Dukes of Devonshire) perhaps explains the enormous 'greenhouse-style' structure that was the Crystal Palace.

Since 1864 members of the Serpentine Swimming Club have raced in the icy waters of the lake every Christmas Day; since 1904 the winner has been awarded the Peter Pan Cup, first presented by *Peter Pan* author J.M. Barrie.

At The Lido café keep straight on along the waterfront until you reach the end of The Serpentine, where you bear slightly right and take the path alongside Rotten Row.

WALK 10 – Knightsbridge, Kensington and a King's Hunting Ground

7 A short way ahead go left into the Rose Garden and through the archway on your right where the perfume in the summer months is wonderful. At the end of the archway go left and straight on past a lamp-post to leave the Rose Garden.

Cross the road, taking the second path on the right and passing a statue of St George and the Dragon. Cross a second road and head straight on to the 7/7 memorial, unveiled in 2009 in tribute to the 52 people who died in the London bombings of 7 July 2005.

This monument commemorates the first Duke's defeat of Napoleon at the Battle of Waterloo in 1815. It was commissioned by George IV in 1825 as a grand entrance to London leading to Buckingham Palace.

Apsley House

In another corner of this site is a memorial dedicated to the British Royal Regiment of Artillery in the First World War. Sculptor Charles Sargeant Jagger served in the Great War and his depiction of a body covered by a greatcoat defied the censorship that banned images of dead British soldiers. Beneath are the words 'Here was a royal fellowship of death', a quote from Shakespeare's *Henry V*.

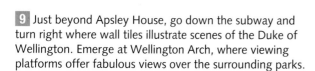

From here, cross the road back to Apsley Gate and go left to Hyde Park Corner Underground. ●

8 Facing the memorial, take the right-hand path, passing a statue of Achilles on your right. Leave the park momentarily on the left so that you can re-enter the park through the colourful Queen Elizabeth Gate, decorated with the heraldic lion and the unicorn and named for the late Queen Mother. Head left through Apsley Gate; to the left is Apsley House, now owned by English Heritage and home to The Wellington Museum. Built in the 18th century, this fine mansion – once home to the first Duke of Wellington – was known as 'Number 1 London', being the first house after the tollgates at the entrance to Knightsbridge.

9 Just beyond Apsley House, go down the subway and turn right where wall tiles illustrate scenes of the Duke of Wellington. Emerge at Wellington Arch, where viewing platforms offer fabulous views over the surrounding parks.

New Zealand comrades

An unusual memorial in the shadow of Wellington Arch is *Southern Stand*, designed by architect John Hardwick-Smith and sculptor Paul Dibble. This structure commemorates the bond between New Zealand and the UK and in particular remembers the antipodean troops who fought in both world wars. Each of the 16 bronze structures is decorated with all things native to New Zealand, including sculptures of wildlife and accompanying inscriptions:

Eaters of honey, honey sweet in song …

WALK 11 – Chelsea Characters and Chic

DISTANCE: 5½ miles (9 kilometres)
START: Sloane Square Underground
END: Sloane Square Underground

Leave Sloane Square Underground where ahead of you, in the centre of Sloane Square, is the bronze Venus fountain, unveiled in 1951 and the result of a competition held by the Royal Academy. From here take the second left on to Lower Sloane Street.

1 Turn left into Pimlico Road with its exclusive antique and furniture shops, cafés and delis. In Orange Square is a statue of child prodigy Mozart who resided nearby as a boy; it was during the short time he lived here that he first met one of his greatest influences, composer Johann Christian Bach (son of Johann Sebastian Bach).

Retrace your steps and cross Lower Sloane Street into Royal Hospital Road. Go left into the grounds of the Royal Chelsea Hospital, world-renowned today as the venue for the annual Chelsea Flower Show. The building, designed by Sir Christopher Wren and with the foundation stone laid by Charles II in 1682, was intended for the 'succour and relief of veterans broken by age and war' and still offers a home and care to old soldiers. Chelsea Pensioners are a familiar sight in London in their distinctive scarlet uniform, first introduced by the Duke of Marlborough in the 18th century.

Royal Chelsea Hospital

2 Passing the old burial grounds on the left you come to the RCH Museum where you can discover how the Chelsea Pensioners live and see many artefacts on display, including The Sovereign's Mace, commissioned for Her Majesty the Queen's Golden Jubilee. From the museum cross to Lighthouse Court and go through the arch in the top right-hand corner; the walls here are lined with memorials. Beyond, in Figure Court, is a gilded statue of Charles II by Grinling Gibbons, portraying the king in Roman costume.

Royal Chelsea Hospital

WALK 11 – Chelsea Characters and Chic

Leave the grounds of the hospital and cross to Franklin's Row immediately opposite which skirts Burton's Court (private grounds owned by the hospital). Turn left into St Leonard's Terrace; on the right is Royal Avenue which along with Burton's Court was laid out by William III in the late 17th century as a carriageway linking the hospital with Kensington Palace. Royal Avenue was the fictional home of Ian Fleming's most famous character, James Bond. It was here in 1968 that Britain's first American-style drugstore opened; the controversial Chelsea Drugstore was immortalized by the Rolling Stones in their song *You Can't Always Get What You Want*, and scenes from Stanley Kubrick's *A Clockwork Orange* were filmed here.

3 Continue on St Leonard's Terrace where you will see a blue plaque to *Dracula* author Bram Stoker. Turn left down Durham Place, which becomes Ormonde Gate, turning right back on to Royal Hospital Road. On the left is the National Army Museum, standing on the site of the one-time home of Sir Robert Walpole, regarded as Britain's first Prime Minister. The canon at the entrance was used during the Crimean War at the Siege of Sebastopol. In the museum you can see the impact the Army has had on the world, with galleries covering warfare from 1066 to 1945 plus changing exhibitions and events.

Go right into Tite Street which was built for access to the Embankment in 1877. Residents of Tite Street have included composer Peter Warlock (No. 30), artists John Singer Sargeant (No. 31), James Abbott McNeill Whistler and, later, Augustus John (No. 33), playwright Oscar Wilde (No. 34) and writer and broadcaster Clement Freud, who lodged at No. 52. Cross Christchurch Street to Tedworth Square where author Mark Twain lived at No. 23.

4 Retrace your steps to turn right into Royal Hospital Road, then left along Swan Walk, named for the Swan Inn mentioned in Pepys' diaries. Here you will find the entrance to the Chelsea Physic Garden, founded in 1673 as the Apothecaries Garden for the cultivation and study of plants for science and medicine. Open on certain days, visitors can enjoy The Historical Walk through the grounds and refreshments at the café here.

5 Keep on Swan Walk and turn right to join Chelsea Embankment, constructed in 1874 and significantly reducing the width of the River Thames. The name 'Chelsea' comes from the Anglo-Saxon meaning 'the landing place for chalk'. Across the river you will see the Peace Pagoda in Battersea Park. Go right along Chelsea Embankment; Chelsea Bridge is behind you and Albert Bridge ahead. Before you get to the bridge go right into Royal Hospital Road; on the left is an entrance to Chelsea Embankment Garden and behind this at No. 4 Cheyne Walk is a plaque to author George Eliot, the pen name of Mary Anne Evans who spent her last days here.

Continue on Royal Hospital Road and go straight over into Flood Street, at one time one of the main shopping streets in Chelsea. A right turn into Robinson Street leads to Christ Church, built in 1839 for the modest sum of £4,000 as a place of worship for the servants employed in the grand houses in the area when Chelsea was a village, separated from the city by open countryside.

6 Return to Flood Street and walk down St Loo Avenue, opposite Robinson Street, turning left to join Chelsea Manor Street and Cheyne Gardens. This part of Chelsea is linked to Henry VIII (look for the blue plaque on the right) who acquired the Manor of Chelsea in 1536, later owned by two men whose names are synonymous with several areas of Chelsea: Lord Charles Cheyne and Sir Hans Sloane.

7 Go right on to Cheyne Walk; as well as George Eliot, numerous famous names have lived here over the years including: David Lloyd George (No. 10); Dante Gabriel Rossetti (No. 16); Mick Jagger (No. 48); Elizabeth Gaskell

Open house

The National Trust's Carlyle's House was a meeting place for Victorian literary greats including Charles Dickens, who was inspired by Thomas Carlyle's work. It was Carlyle's neighbour, writer and poet Leigh Hunt, on whom Dickens is said to have based the optimistically childlike character Harold Skimpole in *Bleak House*. Controversial social commentator Carlyle was himself responsible for many thought-provoking observations, such as:

Speech is human, silence is divine, yet also brutish and dead; therefore we must learn both arts.

Carlyle's House

(No. 93); J.M.W. Turner (No. 119); Sylvia Pankhurst (No. 120). Shortly you come to the statue of *The Boy with the Dolphin* by David Wynne (whose son was the model); to your right is the entrance to Oakley Street where explorer Robert Falcon Scott, fashion designer Mary Quant and musician David Bowie have lived. Cross opposite the dolphin statue to Albert Bridge, opened in 1873 and where at the entrance is a sign ordering troops to break step while crossing to avoid damage to the structure from all those marching feet.

'The Boy with the Dolphin'

Cross back over the road and go left; at the statue of Thomas Carlyle turn right to Cheyne Row and Carlyle's House, home to the Scottish essayist and historian, and his wife Jane. The house and gardens, now in the care of the National Trust, are open to the public.

8 Just beyond is the Catholic Church of Our Most Holy Redeemer, dedicated to St Thomas More; a relic of his vertebrae is kept on the altar. More lived in Chelsea from 1524 and it was from here that he was taken to the Tower of London to be executed in 1535. The church stands on the site of the Orange House, from which the ceramic artist William de Morgan, who lived at No. 8, once ran his business.

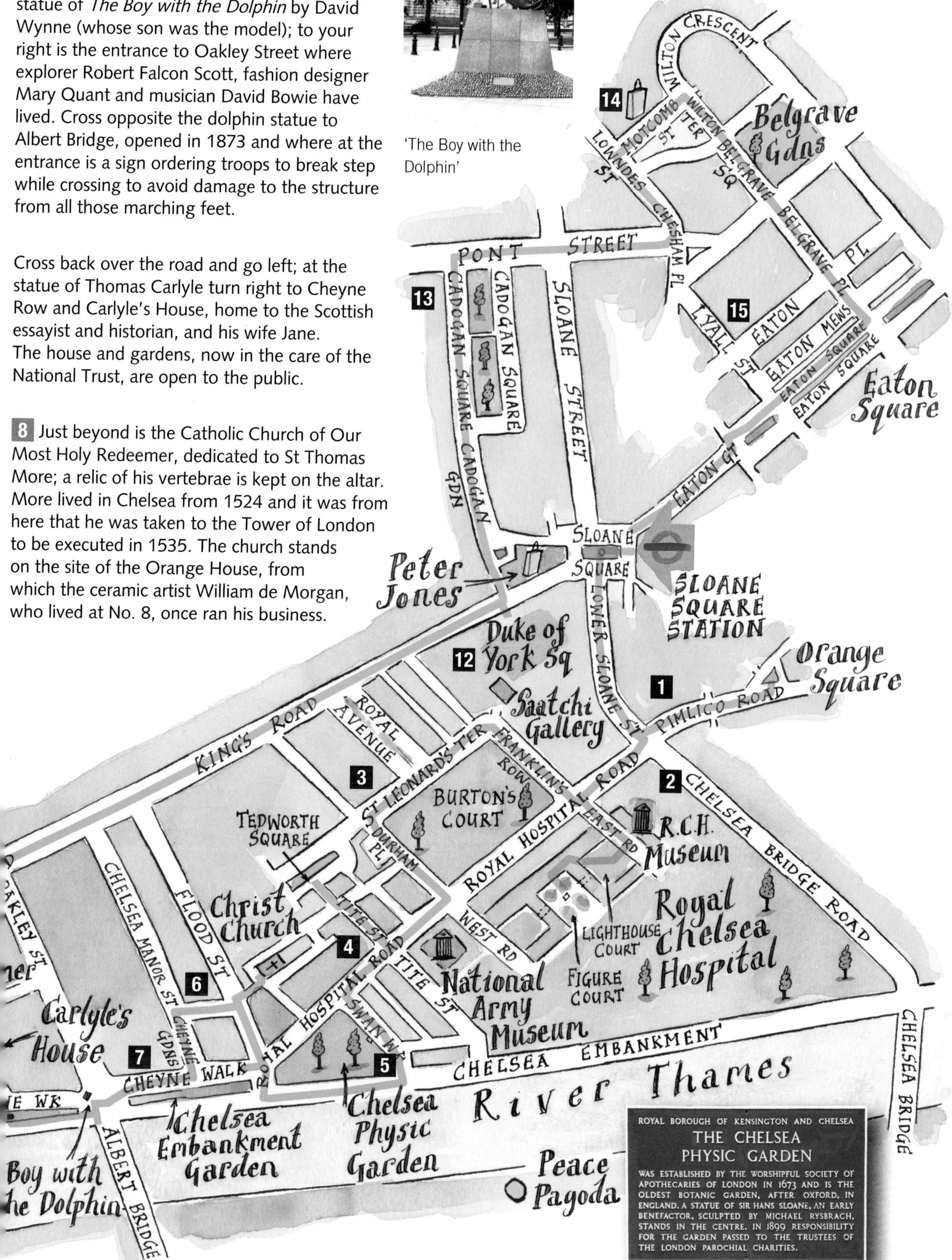

ROYAL BOROUGH OF KENSINGTON AND CHELSEA

THE CHELSEA PHYSIC GARDEN

WAS ESTABLISHED BY THE WORSHIPFUL SOCIETY OF APOTHECARIES OF LONDON IN 1673 AND IS THE OLDEST BOTANIC GARDEN, AFTER OXFORD, IN ENGLAND. A STATUE OF SIR HANS SLOANE, AN EARLY BENEFACTOR, SCULPTED BY MICHAEL RYSBRACH, STANDS IN THE CENTRE. IN 1899 RESPONSIBILITY FOR THE GARDEN PASSED TO THE TRUSTEES OF THE LONDON PAROCHIAL CHARITIES.

Go left to Upper Cheyne Row and left again into Lawrence Street. There are several places of note in this little street: the Chelsea Porcelain Works were on this site, making the distinctive anchor-marked Chelsea China from 1745–84 before moving to Derby; Carlyle Mansions have been home to several famous writers including Henry James, T.S. Eliot, Somerset Maugham and Ian Fleming; the Cross Keys pub at the end, dating from 1765, was a regular haunt of Welsh poet Dylan Thomas.

Tiles in Old Church Street

From the Cross Keys go back along Lawrence Street and left into Justice Walk which brings you to Old Church Street. Look for the Old Dairy with its decorated wall tiles, a reminder of the dairy that once stood here, and the cow's head on the red-brick building behind it.

9 Continue along Old Church Street and cross King's Road. Turn left into Mallord Street where residents have included Welsh artist Augustus John (No. 28) and A.A. Milne (No. 13), legendary author of *Winnie the Pooh*; it was in this house that his son, Christopher Robin, was born.

10 Opposite the Russian House at the end, turn right on to The Vale and right again on to Mulberry Walk with its eclectic mix of houses. Go left back on to Old Church Street. At its junction with Elm Park Road is a blue plaque to William de Morgan; cross here into Carlyle Square, at one time home to Kim Philby who was part of the 'Cambridge Spy Ring' in the 1940s and 50s, and fled to Moscow in 1963. More blue plaques to look for here are those to actress Dame Sybil Thorndike and writer Sir Osbert Sitwell.

11 Rejoin King's Road; turn left and continue along here enjoying the shops, bars and restaurants. One can now only imagine the era when Charles II had the road built as a private thoroughfare between Whitehall and Hampton Court – and until 1830 only those who held a special token with the king's head were permitted to use it.

The King's Road came into its own in the mid-20th century when Mary Quant opened her shop Bazaar here in 1955. The area developed further in the 1960s with numerous boutiques and restaurants frequented by the ultra fashionable and famous, culminating with the punk movement in the 1970s when the shop at No. 430 was owned by Malcolm McLaren and Vivienne Westwood; in fact Dame Vivienne's designer clothes are still sold here.

There is lots of interest to look out for, including the old burial ground at Dovehouse Green, the neo-classical Old Town Hall, the Chelsea Potter pub (frequented by Jim Morrison of the Doors in the 1960s) and, opposite, the grand entrance to The Pheasantry (and Pizza Express) where pheasants were once reared for the royal kitchens. A blue plaque announces that Russian ballerina Princess Astafiev opened a dance academy here in 1916; her most famous pupil was Peggy Hookham, who went on to become Dame Margot Fonteyn.

12 A little further on, on the right, is Duke of York Square with its statue of Hans Sloane, fountains and entrance to the Saatchi Gallery in the former Duke of York's Barracks, plus shops and restaurants in a pleasant pedestrianized area.

Opposite is the famous Peter Jones department store, started by a young Welsh draper who arrived in London in 1864; the store bearing his name has been on King's Road since 1877. Cross here to Cadogan Gardens and continue straight on to Cadogan Square, one-time home of novelist Arnold Bennett.

13 Turn right to Pont Street, passing Langtry's restaurant with its blue plaque to Edward VII's 'official mistress', actress Lillie Langtry, who lived here. She captivated the king with her violet eyes and sense of humour and impressed him with her knowledge of a wide range of topics. Cross Sloane Street, continuing along Pont Street, and go left into Chesham Place which becomes Lowndes Street.

14 A right turn to Motcomb Street (with Christian Louboutin on the corner) leads to exclusive shops and restaurants. At the next junction look left to see the fine sweep of Regency buildings in Wilton Crescent (where Earl Mountbatten of Burma lived at No. 2) but go right along Wilton Terrace. At the end keep right and cross West Halkin Street to Belgrave Square where flags announce the foreign embassies here. Keep right of the gardens in the square and go straight on to Belgrave Place.

15 Cross Eaton Place – the Edwardian setting for the popular 1970s TV drama *Upstairs Downstairs* – and turn right on to Eaton Square; as you pass by these fine houses it is easy to picture the scenes below stairs when game hung in the larder and cook whipped up delicious puddings, while upstairs a butler served afternoon tea to the master and mistress of the house in the drawing room. Famous residents of the square have included politicians – and subsequently Prime Ministers – Stanley Baldwin and Margaret Thatcher.

Head across Lyall Street and continue on Eaton Square, going left at the top. A right turn along Eaton Gate leads back to Sloane Square and the Underground. ●

WALK 12 – A Princely Path to Primrose Hill

DISTANCE: 4½ miles (7 kilometres)
START: Baker Street Underground
END: Regent's Park Underground

Leave Baker Street Underground (with its wall tiles depicting Sherlock Holmes) via the Marylebone Road exit where to your left you can see a statue of the detective. Just beyond the entrance to the Underground, turn right on to Baker Street.

1 At the end on the left is the Sherlock Holmes Museum, where you may catch sight of a 'Victorian policeman' on duty. The museum is packed full of memorabilia concerning Sir Arthur Conan Doyle's most famous literary figure.

2 From here turn right into Allsop Place then left into Marylebone Road where Madame Tussaud's is on the corner. The roots of this famous waxwork attraction date back to 1770 Paris, where the young Madame Tussaud was learning to make wax masks, later including the death masks of aristocrats executed during the French Revolution. She came to Britain in the early 19th century with a travelling exhibition of revolutionary artefacts. The exhibition made a more permanent home in Baker Street in 1835, moving round the corner to Marylebone Road in 1884.

Continue along Marylebone Road where on the right is St Marylebone Parish Church with its fine cupola. Charles Dickens' son was baptized here, an event referred to in his novel *Dombey and Son*.

3 Turn left opposite the church along York Gate that leads into Regent's Park where there is much to see and do, plus cafés to take refreshments.

The vast, round park (it covers over 400 acres/ 160 hectares) sits on what was originally forest land, claimed by Henry VIII as hunting ground in 1538 and becoming known as Marylebone Park. It was developed into the area seen today in the 19th century by John Nash, architect and friend of the Prince Regent, later King George IV.

Regent's Park is referred to in Dodie Smith's book *The Hundred and One Dalmatians*: the dogs lived on the edge of the park and this is where they took their owners for walks. The park has also appeared in several films, including *Brief Encounter* in 1945.

As you enter the park keep straight ahead, following signs for Queen Mary's Garden and the Open Air Theatre. Head over York Bridge, passing Regent's College on your left; in the 19th century this was the site of an observatory from where several minor planets were discovered.

Regent's Park drinking fountain

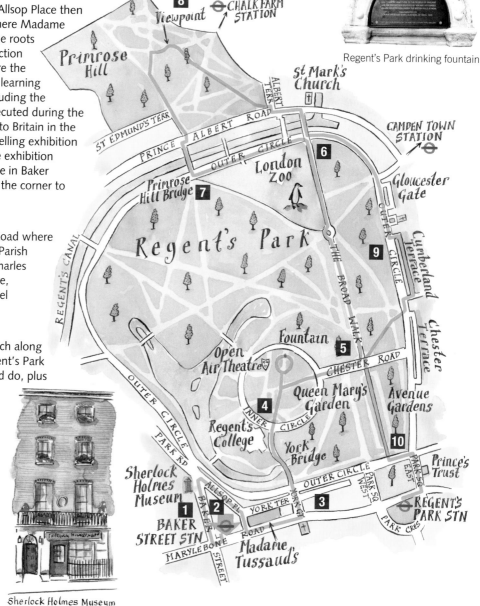

Sherlock Holmes Museum

WALK 12 – A Princely Path to Primrose Hill

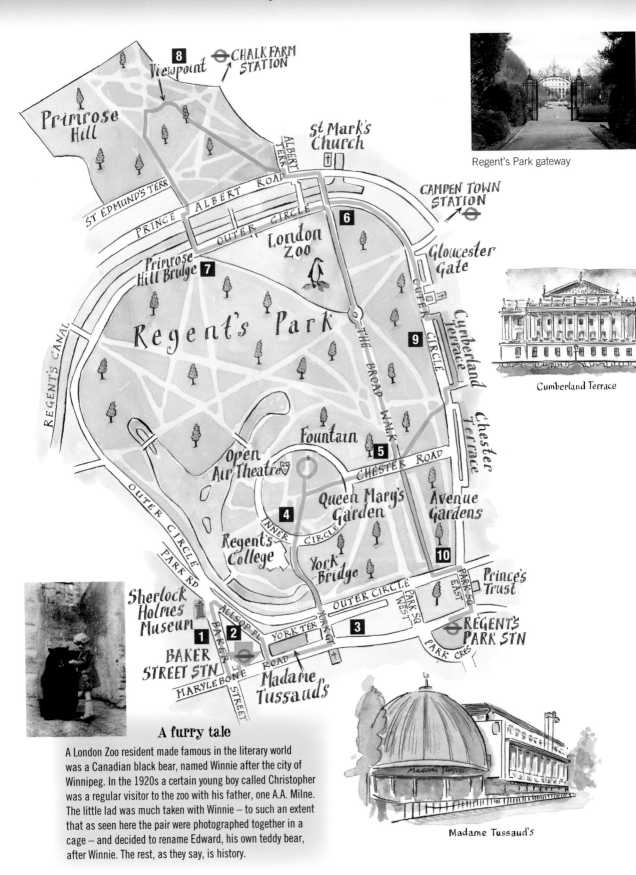

Regent's Park gateway

Cumberland Terrace

Madame Tussaud's

A furry tale

A London Zoo resident made famous in the literary world was a Canadian black bear, named Winnie after the city of Winnipeg. In the 1920s a certain young boy called Christopher was a regular visitor to the zoo with his father, one A.A. Milne. The little lad was much taken with Winnie – to such an extent that as seen here the pair were photographed together in a cage – and decided to rename Edward, his own teddy bear, after Winnie. The rest, as they say, is history.

4 Cross the Inner Circle and go through Jubilee Gates to Queen Mary's Garden, created in the 1930s and named after the wife of George V. Ted Hughes and his wife, Sylvia Plath, lived at Primrose Hill and the garden features in her poem 'Queen Mary's Rose Garden':

> ... In the centre of the garden named after Queen Mary.
> The great roses, many of them scentless,
> Rule their beds like beheaded and resurrected and all
> silent royalty ...

Head for the fountain at the far end, passing the Open Air Theatre on your left. The theatre has been here since 1932, when the first play staged was Shakespeare's *Twelfth Night*.

From the fountain retrace your steps a short way and almost opposite the theatre turn left where you will see a gateway ahead. Go through the gate and cross the Inner Circle into Chester Road.

5 Turn left by the zebra crossing on to The Broad Walk and towards London Zoo. The Broad Walk appears several times in *Mrs Dalloway*, one of Virginia Woolf's most popular novels: '... he remembered Regent's Park; the long straight walk ... an absurd statue with an inscription somewhere or other.'

Head past the grand drinking fountain – possibly the 'statue' referred to above – with its inscription advising that it was erected by the Metropolitan Drinking Fountain and Cattle Trough Association as a gift from a wealthy Parsee Gentleman of Bombay. It was inaugurated by Princess Mary, Duchess of Teck (a cousin of Queen Victoria) in 1869.

6 Leave the park and go left on to the Outer Circle where you will find the entrance to London Zoo. The zoo was founded in 1826 and was the world's first scientific zoo for 'teaching and elucidating zoology'. It opened to the public in 1848 and is now home to over 750 species of animals.

Like his wife, Ted Hughes found inspiration in the area; a London Zoo wolf gets a mention in his poem 'Wolfwatching':

> Woolly-bear white, the old wolf
> Is listening to London ...

7 Carry on past the zoo, catching glimpses of some of the animals as you continue your walk. Cross the road and take the first path on the right over Primrose Hill Bridge that spans Regent's Canal and leads to Prince Albert Road. Go right and cross at the zebra crossing into Primrose Hill. At one time another part of Henry VIII's hunting ground, it is named for the spring flower that grew in abundance in this small London park in the 17th century.

View from Primrose Hill

It is on Primrose Hill that Pongo in *The Hundred and One Dalmatians* engaged in 'twilight barking'. The park also features as the site of a Martian encampment in H. G. Wells' classic *The War of the Worlds*, and appears in the opening scene of the film *Bridget Jones: The Edge of Reason*. Once in the park, follow the path on the left, carrying straight on where the paths cross (St Edmund's Terrace is on the left). Where the path forks, keep right; at the next fork continue right to reach the viewpoint where you can enjoy lovely views over the city and spot many famous landmarks.

8 From the viewpoint, take the path down the hill, leaving the park by the red phone box on the corner of Albert Terrace. Cross Prince Albert Road and head left. Opposite St Mark's Church, turn right over St Mark's Bridge to cross the canal with its narrow boats, an area referred to by Charles Dickens in *The Uncommercial Traveller*, a collection of literary sketches and reminiscences.

Turn left on to the Outer Circle, passing the Nash-designed buildings at Gloucester Gate with their beautiful red and white triangular pediment. Continue past the Danish Church. Originally known as St Katharine's College Chapel, it was granted to the Danish community by Alexandra, the Copenhagen-born queen of Edward VII.

9 Go left into Cumberland Terrace to admire the most elaborate of the Nash-built Regency terraces around the park, with its columns and pediments of white figures and spectacular blue and white triangular central pediment.

Leave Cumberland Terrace to rejoin the Outer Circle. Re-enter Regent's Park through the gateway opposite Chester Terrace, and bear diagonally left to rejoin The Broad Walk. Cross Chester Road and go straight on through Avenue Gardens with its fountains on both sides, where it is easy to imagine London society strolling in Regency times.

10 Head through the gate at the end of the gardens on to the Outer Circle once more. Turn left then right on to Park Square East, passing the Diorama on your left; built in 1823 by Augustus Pugin, the building now houses The Prince's Trust, the charity founded by Prince Charles in 1976.

Go through the gateway and cross Marylebone Road. Bear right and Regent's Park Underground is just ahead of you. ●

WALK 13 – Strolling the South Bank

DISTANCE: 4½ miles (7 kilometres)
START: Westminster Underground
END: Tower Hill Underground

Leave the station following the signs for Embankment, and bear right up the steps where you are greeted by the fine sight of Big Ben and the Houses of Parliament ahead of you, and on your left the statue of Boudicca and her two daughters in a scythed war chariot.

1 Head on to Westminster Bridge; the original dated from 1750 and was replaced in 1862 making the structure you see today the oldest bridge in use in London. As you cross the River Thames you might reflect on the not entirely dissimilar view seen by William Wordsworth in 1802, as immortalized in his poem 'Upon Westminster Bridge':

Ships, towers, domes, theatres, and temples lie
Open unto the fields, and to the sky,
All bright and glittering in the smokeless air.

2 Once on the South Bank, turn left down the steps on to the Thames Path. This stretch of the Thames Path, as far as Tower Bridge, is known as The Queen's Walk. The building on the right is County Hall, opened in 1922 by King George V. Within its walls are several visitor attractions including the London Aquarium and the Dali Universe exhibition.

Continue on the Thames Path passing several imposing Dali sculptures on the way to the London Eye, opposite Jubilee Gardens. The London Eye is an unmissable landmark erected to celebrate the millennium and 'flying the Eye' offers fabulous views over the city.

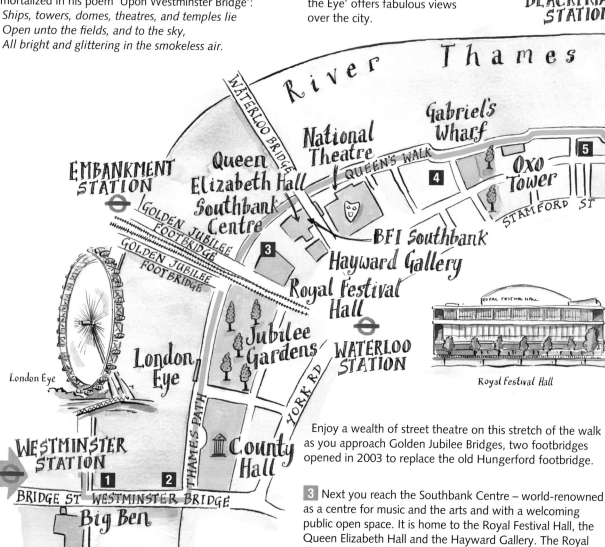

London Eye

Royal Festival Hall

Enjoy a wealth of street theatre on this stretch of the walk as you approach Golden Jubilee Bridges, two footbridges opened in 2003 to replace the old Hungerford footbridge.

3 Next you reach the Southbank Centre – world-renowned as a centre for music and the arts and with a welcoming public open space. It is home to the Royal Festival Hall, the Queen Elizabeth Hall and the Hayward Gallery. The Royal Festival Hall has been redeveloped in the 21st century but was originally built for the Festival of Britain in 1951, which aimed to raise spirits and promote rebuilding in the aftermath of the Second World War. The Queen Elizabeth Hall and the Hayward Gallery first opened in the 1960s.

...ontinue along the Thames Path, passing the BFI Southbank – formerly the National Film Theatre – where a diverse ...ange of films is shown and film festivals are held.

...ass under Waterloo Bridge, named for the British victory ...n the 1815 battle. The first river crossing on this site was ...he Strand Bridge, a toll bridge opened in 1817; the current ...ridge was completed in 1945. Immediately past the ...ridge is the National Theatre, home of the Royal National ...heatre Company, with its varied programme of classic and ...ontemporary productions.

5 The next river crossing you come to is Blackfriars Bridge. The one you see today dates from 1869 but the first bridge here, originally called Pitt Bridge, opened in 1769 and for several years foot passengers had to pay a halfpenny (and one penny on Sundays) to cross it. As you pass under its arches you will see scenes of the bridge in years gone by depicted on wall tiles.

Between Blackfriars Bridge and the Millennium Bridge sits Tate Modern; created in 2000 in the former Bankside Power Station, it displays British and international art from 1900.

6 Climb the steps of Millennium Bridge for a spectacular view of St Paul's Cathedral over the river. The bridge was built as the result of an international competition; it opened in June 2000 but closed two days later to much controversy because it swayed under the large numbers of people using it; after modifications it reopened in 2002.

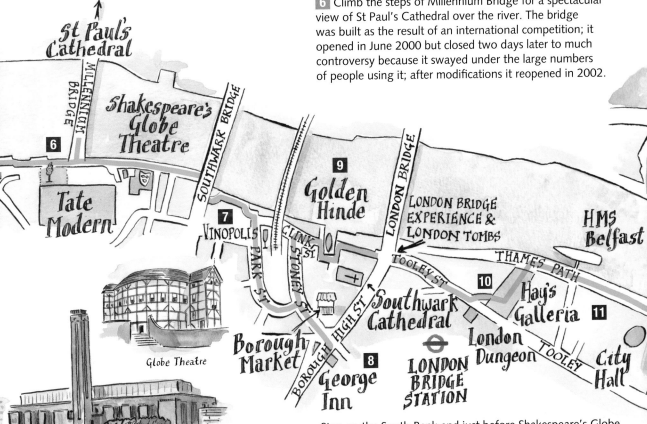

Globe Theatre

Tate Modern

4 In the distance over the water you will see the dome of St Paul's Cathedral, Sir Christopher Wren's masterpiece dating from the 17th century, and the iconic Gherkin, completed in 2004. As you reach Gabriel's Wharf look up to see another famous London landmark, the Oxo Tower. The tower, once owned by the company who made the famous stock cubes, was cleverly designed to avoid the one-time ban on sky-high advertising. The building was redeveloped in the 1990s as designer apartments, retail outlets and a rooftop restaurant. Take the lift to a public viewing gallery for a great view over the river.

Stay on the South Bank and just before Shakespeare's Globe Theatre notice two ancient houses tucked away: Provost's Lodging (the provost in this instance being the Dean of nearby Southwark Cathedral) and Cardinal's Wharf, with a plaque claiming that Christopher Wren resided here while St Paul's Cathedral was being built.

Shakespeare's Globe is a reconstruction of the original that burned down in 1613 'all in less than two hours', and was the first building in the city to have a thatched roof following a ban after the Great Fire of London in 1666. Situated less than 650 feet (200 metres) from the site of the old Globe Theatre, the new structure was completed in 1997, thanks to a project championed by American actor and film producer Sam Wanamaker.

WALK 13 – Strolling the South Bank

Head under Southwark Bridge, first opened in 1819 and rebuilt in 1921. Just past the Anchor pub turn right to Bank End and Vinopolis where you can dine and enjoy wine-tasting tours under Victorian railway arches.

7 With Vinopolis on your left go straight on into Park Street. Follow the road round and you will see Borough Market ahead of you. The market has been on this site since the 18th century, though one has been held on the South Bank for many centuries. To ease congestion in the 16th century women selling goods from baskets were not allowed to stop walking so continually had to 'cry their wares' as they made their way through the stalls. Turn right at the Market Porter pub into Stoney Street.

8 Cross Southwark Street at the crossing just to your left and bear right into Borough High Street. Tucked away on the left is the 17th-century George Inn; restored by the National Trust it is the last remaining galleried hostelry in London. Customers here have included William Shakespeare, who wrote many of his plays while living in Southwark, and

Charles Dickens, whose father was sent to a nearby debtors prison. Dickens' subsequently set *Little Dorrit* in the area an The George is mentioned fleetingly in the story.

Return to Stoney Street and head straight down to Clink Street where on your left is Clink Prison Museum. The museum is on the site where a prison stood from 860 AD to 1780, and is thought to be named for the noise made by the prisoners' chains – hence the term 'in the clink' as slang for being in prison.

Southwark Cathedral

For over 1,000 years Christians have worshipped here:

AD 606 - a convent
AD 1106 - a priory
AD 1540 - a parish church
AD 1905 - a cathedral

The oldest gothic church building in London. Gower, Chaucer, Shakespeare, Massinger, Fletcher, Alleyn, Jonson, Harvard, Bishop Andrewes and Dickens are among those associated with this church.

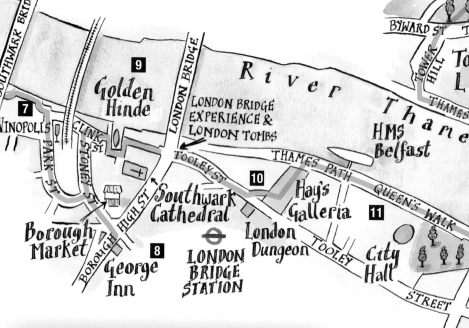

Frost fairs

As you pass under Southwark Bridge you can see slate etchings by sculptor Richard Kindersley of the London frost fairs, first recorded in 1608 and held when the Thames froze in the depths of winter. Until the early 19th century the river was wider and shallower and the narrow arches of London Bridge hampered its flow, causing the water to freeze more easily. During the Great Frost of 1683–84, the river was frozen for two months, the ice measuring up to 11 inches (28cms) thick.

Behold the liquid Thames frozen o're ...

Tower Bridge

To the right of Stoney Street, at Pickfords Wharf, are the remains of Winchester Palace, built in 1107 as a residence for the Bishop of Winchester and remaining as such until the 17th century.

9 Ahead is the *Golden Hinde*, a replica of Sir Francis Drake's 16th-century galleon, where visitors can experience what life was like for Elizabethan sailors.

Follow the road round to the entrance to Southwark Cathedral, on a site where a church has stood for over 1,000 years. The cathedral has links to Shakespeare, with a memorial depicting the playwright reclining, a stained-glass window showing characters from his plays, and, near the choir stalls, a commemorative paving stone to his brother who is buried here.

Just before London Bridge is The Mudlark, a pub that has appeared in several films including 2001's *Bridget Jones's Diary*. Continue under London Bridge; the current river crossing was opened in 1973 but one has stood near here since Roman times. The bridge is referred to by Charles Dickens in *Great Expectations, David Copperfield* and *Oliver Twist*. In the latter, Nancy had a meeting (which ultimately led to her death) on steps by the bridge, which became known as Nancy's Steps.

Beneath the bridge are The London Bridge Experience and the London Tombs, where special effects and actors bring old London to life, and a creepy trip takes you into the ancient vaults of the famous bridge. Carry straight on under the bridge; over the road on Tooley Street (next to London Bridge station) is The London Dungeon – an interactive experience of scary events in the city's history.

10 Opposite The London Dungeon go left into Middle Yard and follow the path to the right to Hay's Galleria, on the site of Hay's Wharf where ships docked until the 1960s. Hay's Galleria has a selection of shops, restaurants – and often exhibitions – and has as its centrepiece a David Kemp sculpture, *The Navigators*.

Rejoin the Thames Path and go right to HMS *Belfast*. The vessel was launched in 1938 and saw much action during the Second World War before retiring from service in the 1960s. Today visitors can enjoy onboard exhibitions and an historic exploration of her nine decks.

11 Continue along the wide Queen's Walk. As you approach Tower Bridge you may see it opening for a ship to pass through, which only happens when a tall vessel pre-arranges it. The domed glass building on your right is City Hall: housing the offices of the Mayor of London and the London Assembly, the building was opened in 2002 and is open to the public.

Go under Tower Bridge on to Shad Thames, passing the Anchor Brewhouse on your left. Notice the bridges above you where dockers transferred goods from the ships to warehouses. Carry straight on to the far end and the Design Museum; its changing exhibitions celebrate design in all forms, from furniture to graphic art and from fashion to architecture.

12 Back at the river, pass waterside restaurants on your return to Tower Bridge. As you climb the steps on to the bridge notice the griffins perched on top of the entrance. Cross the bridge to the Tower Bridge Exhibition where as well as learning how the structure operates you can visit the engine rooms and enjoy panoramic views from the walkways.

13 Once over the river, go down the steps and left under the bridge. Rejoin the Thames Path and pass the Tower of London with its red-coated Yeoman Warders, legendary ravens, priceless Crown Jewels – and, possibly, the ghost of a bear owned by either Henry III or George III.

Follow the path round to the right up Tower Hill and cross Byward Street into Trinity Square Gardens. Leave the gardens on the right where steps lead up to a giant sundial. Beyond on the right is the entrance to Tower Hill Underground, and just past this on the left you might like to see part of London Wall dating from AD 200. ●

City Hall and Tower Bridge

WALK 14 – A Pirate's Path to Docklands

DISTANCE: 4½ miles (7 kilometres)
START: Tower Hill Underground
END: Canary Wharf Underground

Exit Tower Hill Underground and head on to Trinity Square Gardens where you can see memorials to seafarers who lost their lives in the Second World War and the Falklands War. The magnificent colonnaded building on the right at No. 10 Trinity Square dates from the 1920s, with statuary representing commerce, navigation, export, produce and Father Thames as symbols of the prosperity borne by the river.

2 Following the signs for the Thames Path and St Katharine Docks you can enjoy the spectacle that is Tower Bridge, dating from 1894. This is the only one of London's bridges across the Thames that opens to allow river traffic to pass through. Go through the archway under the bridge and bear slightly left to St Katharine Docks. Opened in 1823 they were at the start of London's Docklands area and part of the Port of London – at that time the world's largest port. The docks here were devastated during the Second World War but renovations started in the 1970s.

Tower of London

Walk alongside the harbour, with The Dickens Inn in front of you. Turn right by the phone box and post box next to Marble Quay and join St Katharine's Way, following the signs for the Thames Path. Pass Millers Wharf Buildings and turn right along the Thames Path to go along Tower Bridge Wharf then rejoin St Katharine's Way, which becomes Wapping High Street.

All Hallows by the Tower

1 Leave the gardens and turn right along Byward Street to the entrance of All Hallows by the Tower, the oldest church in the City of London with origins dating back to 675 AD. It was from the tower of the church that Samuel Pepys, who lived in Seething Lane opposite, watched London burn during the Great Fire of 1666; Pepys helped to save the church from the flames.

Leaving the church, retrace your steps a short way, passing a dragon marking the boundary of the 'square mile' that is the City of London as you approach the Tower of London. Turn right along the paved Tower Hill leading down to the Tower of London; built by William the Conqueror to protect the city at this vantage point on the River Thames, it is rich in royal and bloody history. Turn left alongside the river past Traitors' Gate through which many prisoners have sailed to their fate, including Henry VIII's second wife, Anne Boleyn, en route to her execution on Tower Green on 19 May 1536.

Wapping is known for the printing and publishing industry following the controversial move in 1986 of Rupert Murdoch's News International from Fleet Street when new technology was introduced.

Walk through Hermitage Riverside Memorial Garden with its Wendy Taylor dove sculpture, then continue along the riverside to Cinnabar Wharf; another Wendy Taylor sculpture here, *Voyager*, was inspired by a ship's propeller. Back on the street you come to the Town of Ramsgate pub where until the early 19th century men, press-ganged to serve on ships and convicts bound for the colonies, were held in the cellar before being led down eerie Wapping Old Stairs to the water.

In Hermitage Riverside Memorial Garden is a beautifully simple dove sculpture by award-winning sculptor Wendy Taylor, dedicated to the civilians of the East End killed or injured in the

London Blitz of 1940–41 when German planes dropped hundreds of bombs on the capital. The garden is built on the site of Hermitage Wharf, destroyed by a firebomb in an air raid on 29 December 1940.

4 Go left in front of New Crane Wharf into Garnet Street, bearing right along Wapping Wall past Jubilee Wharf to The Prospect of Whitby pub. In the 17th century it was a meeting place for smugglers and villains, and became known as 'Devil's Tavern'. It was rebuilt following a fire in the 18th century and renamed after a ship moored nearby. Go upstairs to the balcony for a great view of Canary Wharf – and a noose swinging over the river, a reminder that the notorious Judge Jeffreys, the 'Hanging Judge', was a regular here.

Prospect of Whitby

3 Opposite the pub is the churchyard of the one-time St John's Church. Walk through here and leave by the gate on the far right; turn right into Scandrett Street where outside the old St John of Wapping School are charming, colourful statues of children and a reminder of how schoolboys and schoolgirls were segregated.

Return to Wapping High Street and go left where you will pass the Marine Policing Unit and the Captain Kidd pub. The pub is near the site of Execution Dock where pirates met their fate and their bodies were chained and left for the tide to wash over them. The infamous William Kidd was hanged here in 1701, and his body left in an iron gibbet cage strung over the river for 20 years as a warning to would-be miscreants.

Opposite the pub is the red-brick London Hydraulic Power Company where water pumped from the Thames provided power for, amongst many other things, raising Tower Bridge and Shadwell Bridge which is just ahead of you. Operations stopped here in 1977 and the building now houses The Wapping Project, a cultural arts venue and restaurant where you can dine amongst the old machinery.

5 Cross Shadwell Bridge and go right along the Thames Path and into King Edward Memorial Park to see the memorial stone to navigators who set sail to explore the seas in the 16th century.

Leave the park and continue along the river to emerge on Narrow Street in Limehouse, the area named for the lime kilns established in the 14th century to produce quicklime. Look along Spert Street to see the entrance to the Rotherhithe Tunnel which runs beneath the river and opened in 1908.

Continue along Narrow Street, going right on to the Thames Path and up the steps next to The Narrow pub. You may have to wait to cross the swing bridge over Limehouse Basin, opened in 1820 as Regent's Canal Dock and the final lock on Regent's Canal.

WALK 14 – A Pirate's Path to Docklands

Follow Narrow Street to The Grapes pub, thought to be The Six Jolly Fellowship Porters in Charles Dickens' *Our Mutual Friend*, which he referred to as being 'of a dropsical appearance … it had not a straight floor and hardly a straight line … with a crazy wooden verandah impending over the water.'

6 Opposite the pub is the *Herring Gull* sculpture by Jane Ackroyd. Beneath the park here runs the busy Limehouse Link roadway. To the left you can see the tower of the Baroque-style St Anne's Church, off Three Colt Street. Completed in 1724, amongst a landscape of what was then open fields, its tower became a landmark for ships docking in the East End. After Big Ben, St Anne's clock tower claims to be the highest in Britain.

At Canary Wharf Pier go left up the steps. Just beyond the main road on the left, and next to No. 1 Westferry Circus, go through the walkway on the left where steps or a lift bring you out on Ontario Way.

8 Turn right here then left to Hertsmere Road, then right opposite Cannon Drive on to West India Quay. West India Docks – London's first purpose-built cargo handling dock – was the result of a project championed by merchant Robert Milligan who grew up on his family's sugar plantations in Jamaica. The docks opened in 1802, importing produce from the West Indies including sugar, coffee and rum, and were considered to be England's greatest civil engineering structure at that time.

On the left of West India Quay is the Museum of London Docklands where, as well as enjoying changing exhibitions, you can explore the history of the city's river and see such things as a gibbet cage, similar to the one in which Captain Kidd's body hung over the river for 20 years.

9 Continue along West India Quay with its bars and restaurants, heading right over the footbridge to Wren's Landing. Cross the road to Cabot Square; turn left at the fountain. Turn right then left along The South Colonnade. Go down steps on the right opposite One Canada Square – at 770-feet (235-metres) high its 50 storeys made it the tallest habitable building in the UK when it was built in 1991 – and carry straight on where you will see the entrance to Canary Wharf Underground on your left. ●

Cross at the junction of Narrow Street and Limehouse Causeway, going right along Three Colt Street and passing Lime Kiln Wharf. Cross at the junction with Milligan Street and follow the signs for the Thames Path.

7 Go left along the river at Canary Riverside with its cafés and restaurants as you enter the area known as Canary Wharf; it takes its name from a cargo warehouse once situated at the heart of the docklands area and linked to the fruit trade with the Canary Islands.

Sculpture in Cabot Square

WALK 15 – Glorious Greenwich

DISTANCE: 4½ miles (7 kilometres)
START: Blackheath Station
END: Blackheath Station

Turn left out of Blackheath Station and make your way down Tranquil Vale with its fantastic choice of cafés, bars and restaurants.

1 Cross Royal Parade on to a gravel path across Blackheath with, on your right, All Saints church, consecrated on All Saints Day (1 November) 1958.

Follow the gravel path and turn right along Duke Humphrey Road, named for the duke who in 1433 was granted a licence to 'empark 200 acres of land, pasture, weed, heath and furze' by his brother, Henry V. Continue across the wide expanse of heathland where Wat Tyler rallied his rebels and met Richard II during the Peasants' Revolt of 1381, in reaction to the introduction of a poll tax that was the same for both rich and poor.

2 Cross the road to Blackheath Gate into Greenwich Park. This is the oldest of the enclosed royal parks and was laid out in the early 1600s; some of the trees from that period are still here today. Walk up the long, straight Blackheath Avenue, passing the Pavilion Tea House on your right. On your left are the buildings of the Royal Observatory and, ahead, a statue of General James Wolfe who lived at Macartney House in the park. Wolfe is famed for his victory at the Battle of Quebec in 1759, where he lost his life. Here is a fine viewpoint overlooking The Queen's House and London landmarks including the O$_2$ arena.

Next to the statue is the entrance to the Royal Observatory. Step inside and follow the 'Meridian route' where amongst many other amazing things you can see a 100-foot (30-metre) deep well where John Flamsteed, the first Astronomer Royal, sat at the bottom to observe the stars. On top of Flamsteed House, the original Observatory building where John Flamsteed lived and worked, is a red time ball dating from 1833, which rises daily at 12.55 and falls at exactly 13.00 GMT. And of course what everyone wants to see (and straddle) is the Greenwich Meridian Line – the Prime Meridian of the World (longitude 0°) which divides the Earth into eastern and western hemispheres in the same way the Equator divides the northern and southern hemispheres.

Time Ball, Flamsteed House

The Queen's House

Isle of Dogs

River Thames

Old Royal Naval College

Pepys Building

Greenwich Pier

Trafalgar Tavern

The Queen's House

MAZE HILL STN

5 Cutty Sark

Gipsy Moth Pub

CUTTY SARK STN

GREENWICH CHURCH ST

6

ROMNEY ROAD

PARK ROW

THAMES PATH

7

BOATING LAKE

8 Vanbrugh Castle

MAZE HILL GATE

One Tree Hill

JUBILEE GATE

ST MARY'S GATE

JUBILEE AVE

Q.E. Oak

Roman Shrine

GREENWICH STATION

St Alfege Church

4

STOCKWELL ST

THE AVENUE

3 Royal Observatory

Wolfe Statue

National Maritime Museum

Fan Museum

CROOMS HILL

Pavilion Tea House

BLACKHEATH AVE

Flower Gdn

BOWER AVE

MAZE HILL

Greenwich Park

Secret Gdn

CHARLTON WAY

Meridian Line

BLACKHEATH GATE

9

SHOOTERS HILL ROAD

SHOOTERS HILL RD

2

Blackheath

GOFFERS ROAD

DUKE HUMPHREY RD

All Saints Church

1

TRANQUIL VALE

ROYAL PARADE

MONTPELIER VALE

10

BLACKHEATH STATION

Royal Observatory

Royal Observatory

WALK 15 – Glorious Greenwich

Following the 'Astronomy route' takes you on an exploration of space: you can see part of the Gibson meteorite which is an incredible 4.5 billion years old, an 18th-century mechanical model of the solar system and an exciting state-of-the-art planetarium.

3 Leave the building and go past the 24-hour Shepherd Gate Clock; dating from 1852 and built by Charles Shepherd, this is the clock that brought about the concept of coordinated time. Head down the slope alongside the clock and when you come to some seats, go right along tree-lined Jubilee Avenue, then left to leave the park through St Mary's Gate.

4 Go left to Nevada Street and left again into Crooms Hill where you will find The Fan Museum with over 3,500 fans from all over the world dating from the 11th century. Go back along Crooms Hill and into Stockwell Street where at the end is St Alfege Church. A place of worship has stood here since the 11th century, and this is where Henry VIII was baptised and General Wolfe is buried.

While in Greenwich it is worth seeking out the Tourist Information Centre where a warm and friendly welcome and a marvellous range of information awaits. Make your way into Greenwich Church Street with its choice of shops; look out for Greenwich Market, where a market has been held since 1737. Head towards the river, passing The Gipsy Moth pub and Cutty Sark Gardens to reach Greenwich Pier. The round building in front of you is the entrance to the foot tunnel which, if you wish to extend your walk, takes you 50 feet (15 metres) beneath the River Thames to the Isle of Dogs.

5 Turn right on to the Thames Path alongside Cutty Sark Gardens, home to the famous tea-clipper *Cutty Sark*. The vessel was launched in Scotland in 1869 and after many decades of service sailing the world she was moved to dry dock here in 1954; a fire in 2007 almost destroyed her but she is being carefully restored.

Walk alongside the river, passing the Pepys Building, Trinity College of Music – from which you might hear a refrain – and the Old Royal Naval College, built on the site of Greenwich Palace, the birthplace of both Henry VIII and Elizabeth I. The Old Royal Naval College, designed by Sir Christopher Wren, was founded in 1694 as the Royal Hospital for Seamen. You can visit the Painted Hall (where Nelson's body lay in state) with its magnificent ceiling, and the neo-classical Chapel of St Peter and St Paul.

Turn right on to Park Row where a statue of Nelson at the Trafalgar Tavern looks out over the water. Built in 1837 this used to be the George Inn and is where naval men rubbed shoulders with the likes of William Gladstone, William Makepeace Thackeray and Charles Dickens. In *Our Mutual Friend*, Dickens' last novel, the characters Bella Wilfer and John Rokesmith dined here on their wedding day.

6 Go along Park Row, crossing and turning right into Romney Road and left into the grounds of The Queen's House, part of the National Maritime Museum. The exquisite Queen's House was commissioned by Anne of Denmark, wife of James I, and designed by Inigo Jones in the 17th century. One of the many wonderful things to be seen here is the Tulip Stairs, the first spiral staircase in Britain; it was here in 1966 that the Reverend Hardy famously took photographs of seemingly ghostly figures.

Next door, the magnificent National Maritime Museum itself was opened to the public by King George VI, accompanied by his daughter Princess Elizabeth, in 1937 and illustrates the importance of Britain's seafaring past through a wealth of collections and changing exhibitions. Amongst other exhibits is the coat (with bullet hole) that Nelson was wearing when he was fatally wounded and a gilded royal barge that was used on the Thames until 1846.

7 Pass through the colonnaded walkway to the far side of The Queen's House and re-enter Greenwich Park through Jubilee Gate in front of the National Maritime Museum's Galleries. Follow the left-hand path through the park and go right in front of the boating lake. Where five paths meet take the second left; a climb leads you to another viewpoint, One Tree Hill. The hill was a favourite spot of Queen Elizabeth I, overlooking Greenwich Palace where the (much-disputed) story says Sir Walter Raleigh laid his cloak over a puddle so that the queen would not muddy her shoes. A carved verse at the hilltop reads:

Here fair Eliza, Virgin Queen, from business free enjoyed the scene …

8 Continue straight on, turning left through Maze Hill Gate to Vanbrugh Castle. Now converted into private apartments, this folly was built by architect and playwright Sir John Vanbrugh who lived here from 1719 to 1726. He modelled it on the Bastille where he was imprisoned for spying in 1690–92.

View from Greenwich Park

Re-enter the park opposite the castle and go straight along the third path, and straight on at the next crossroads to the remains of the Queen Elizabeth oak, planted in the 12th century. From here go left and left again on to Bower Avenue and the site of a Roman shrine (you'll have to use your imagination).

Tumbling down One Tree Hill

One Tree Hill in Greenwich Park has always been a popular spot for artists to record the view. In his 1811 comic etching, Thomas Rowlandson portrays the public holiday pastime of 'tumbling' that used to take place here. Young men loved the hazardous sport and so too did some of their female companions — somewhat surprising as they had to risk showing far more than was modest as they tumbled, often breaking limbs in the process.

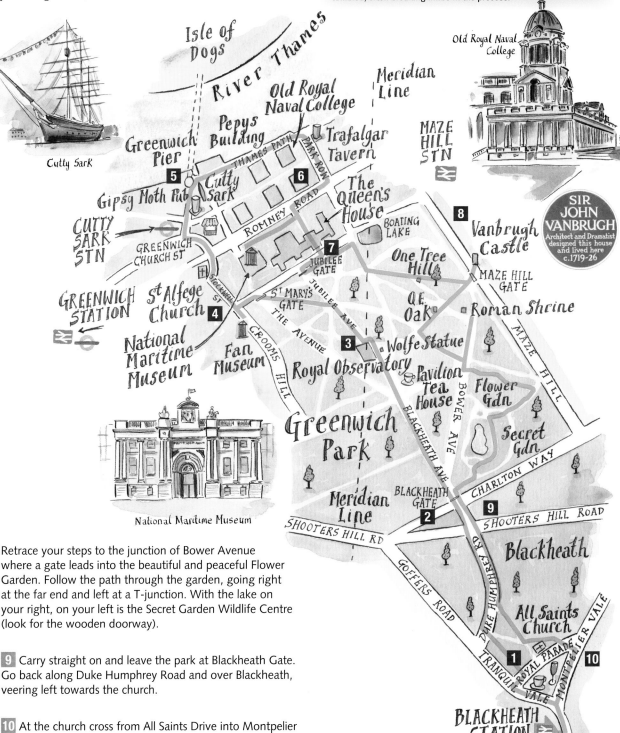

Cutty Sark

National Maritime Museum

Retrace your steps to the junction of Bower Avenue where a gate leads into the beautiful and peaceful Flower Garden. Follow the path through the garden, going right at the far end and left at a T-junction. With the lake on your right, on your left is the Secret Garden Wildlife Centre (look for the wooden doorway).

9 Carry straight on and leave the park at Blackheath Gate. Go back along Duke Humphrey Road and over Blackheath, veering left towards the church.

10 At the church cross from All Saints Drive into Montpelier Vale. Turn right then left back on to Tranquil Vale and make your way to Blackheath Station. ●

Visitor Information

Some visitor sites are not open all year round and in all instances the days/times of opening and entry fees vary – and pre-booking may be necessary – so please check before visiting; websites and phone numbers are given here.

Where entry to museums, galleries and other visitor attractions is free, this is indicated below – although donations are generally encouraged and welcomed, and there is often a charge for special exhibitions. Clearly entry charges will not apply for certain sites listed, such as parks, shops and most churches. Entry to venues such as theatres or concert halls is usually only available when seeing a show, although tours may be available – check websites for details.

All Hallows by the Tower Church: www.ahbtt.org.uk, 020 7481 2928

All Saints Church, Blackheath: www.allsaintsblackheath.org

Apsley House: www.apsleyhouseguide.co.uk, 020 7499 5676. Entry charge

Atlantis Bookshop: www.theatlantisbookshop.com, 020 7405 2120

Bank of England Museum: www.bankofengland.co.uk/education/museum, 020 7601 5545. Free

Barbican Centre: www.barbican.org.uk, 020 7638 4141

Banqueting House: www.hrp.org.uk/banquetinghouse, 0844 482 7777. Entry charge (free for under 16s)

BFI Southbank: www.bfi.org.uk, 020 7928 3535

British Museum: www.britishmuseum.org, 020 7323 8000/8299. Free

* Buckingham Palace: www.royalcollection.org.uk and follow the links. Entry charge (free for under 5s)

Cabinet War Rooms and Churchill Museum: http://cwr.iwm.org.uk, 020 7930 6961. Entry charge (free for under 16s)

Captain Kidd pub: 020 7480 5759

Carlyle's House: www.nationaltrust.org.uk/main/w-carlyleshouse, 020 7352 7087. Entry charge

Catholic Church of Our Most Holy Redeemer and St Thomas More, Chelsea: www.rcdow.org.uk/chelsea2, 020 7352 0777

Charles Dickens Museum: www.dickensmuseum.com, 020 7405 2127. Entry charge

Chelsea Physic Garden: www.chelseaphysicgarden.co.uk, 020 7352 5646. Entry charge (free for under 5s)

Chelsea Potter pub: 020 7352 9479

Christ Church, Chelsea: www.chelseaparish.org, 020 7351 7365

Christian Louboutin: www.christianlouboutin.com, 020 7245 6510

City Hall: www.london.gov.uk/gla/city_hall, 020 7983 4000. Free

* Clarence House: www.royalcollection.org.uk and follow the links. Entry charge (free for under 5s)

Clink Prison Museum: www.clink.co.uk, 020 7403 0900. Entry charge

Connaught Hotel: www.the-connaught.co.uk, 020 7499 7070

Counting House pub: 08721 077 077

County Hall: www.londoncountyhall.com, events line 020 7981 2555

Courtauld Gallery: www.courtauld.ac.uk/gallery, 020 7848 2526. Entry charge (free for under 18s)

Criterion Theatre: www.criterion-theatre.co.uk, box office 0844 847 1778

Cross Keys pub: www.thexkeys.co.uk, 020 7349 9111

Cutty Sark: www.cuttysark.org.uk, 020 8858 2698. Entry charge

Danish Church: www.danskekirke.org, 020 7935 7584

Design Museum: http://designmuseum.org, 020 7403 6933. Entry charge (free for under 12s)

Dickens Inn: www.dickensinn.co.uk, 020 7488 2208

Dominion Theatre: www.dominiontheatre.co.uk, central booking line 0870 124 9127

Dr Johnson's House: www.drjohnsonshouse.org, 020 7353 3745. Entry charge

English Chapel of Christ the King, Gordon Square: www.fifparish.com/home/christtheking, 020 7388 3588

Fan Museum: www.fan-museum.org, 020 8305 1441/020 8293 1889. Entry charge (free for under 7s)

Fortnum & Mason: www.fortnumandmason.com, 020 7734 8040

Garrick Theatre: www.garrick-theatre.co.uk, central booking line 0870 124 9127

George Inn: 020 7407 2056

Gipsy Moth pub: www.thegipsymothgreenwich.co.uk, 020 8858 0786

Gordon's Wine Bar: www.gordonswinebar.com, 020 7930 1408

The Grapes pub: 020 7987 4396

Gray's Inn Chapel: www.graysinn.info and follow link for the chapel, 020 7402 4937

Green Park: www.royalparks.org.uk/parks/green_park, 020 7298 2000

Greenwich Park: www.royalparks.org.uk/parks/greenwich_park, 020 7298 2000

Greenwich Tourist Information Centre: www.greenwichwhs.org.uk, 0870 608 2000

Guards Chapel: www.guards-shop.com/chapel.htm, 020 7414 3229

Guards Museum: www.theguardsmuseum.com, 020 7414 3271/3428. Entry charge (free for under 16s)

Golden Hinde: www.goldenhinde.com, 020 7403 0123. Entry charge

Guildhall: www.guildhall.cityoflondon.gov.uk, 020 7606 3030

Guildhall Art Gallery & Roman London's Amphitheatre: www.cityoflondon.gov.uk/Corporation/LGNL_Services/Leisure_and_culture/Museums_and_galleries/Guildhall_Art_Gallery, 020 7332 3700. Entry charge (free for under 16s; see website for other free concessions)

Hamleys: www.hamleys.com, 0871 704 1977

Harrods: www.harrods.com/harrodsstore, 020 7730 1234

Hatchards Bookshop, Piccadilly: www.hatchards.co.uk, 020 7439 9921

Her Majesty's Theatre Haymarket: www.hermajestys.co.uk, central booking line 0870 124 9127

HMS Belfast: http://hmsbelfast.iwm.org.uk, 020 7940 6300. Entry charge (free for under 16s)

Holy Trinity Church, Brompton: www.htb.org.uk, 0845 644 7533/020 7052 0200

Household Cavalry Museum: www.householdcavalrymuseum.co.uk, 020 7930 3070. Entry charge (free for under 5s)

Houses of Parliament: www.parliament.uk. Free but pre-bookings required for most options (see website)

Hyde Park: www.royalparks.org.uk/parks/hyde_park, 020 7298 2000

Institute of Contemporary Art: www.ica.org.uk, 020 7930 0493. Free

James Smith and Sons, Umbrella and Stick Stores: www.james-smith.co.uk, 020 7836 4731

Kensington Gardens: www.royalparks.org.uk/parks/kensington_gardens, 020 7298 2000

Kensington Palace: www.hrp.org.uk/kensingtonPalace, 0844 482 7777. Entry charge (free for under 5s)

The Lamb pub: 020 7405 0713

Langtry's Restaurant: www.langtrysrestaurant.com, 020 7201 6619

Liberty: www.liberty.co.uk, 020 7734 1234

Lincoln's Inn Chapel: www.lincolnsinn.org.uk and follow link for the chapel; 020 7405 1393

London Bridge Experience and London Tombs: www.thelondonbridgeexperience.com, 0800 0434 666. Entry charge

London Dungeon: www.thedungeons.com/en/london-dungeon/index.html, 020 7234 8675. Entry charge

London Palladium: www.london-palladium.co.uk, central booking line 0870 124 9127

London Transport Museum: www.ltmuseum.co.uk, 020 7379 6344. Entry charge (free for under 16s)

London Zoo: www.zsl.org/zsl-london-zoo, 020 7722 3333. Entry charge (free for under 3s)

Madame Tussaud's: www.madametussauds.com/london, 0871 894 3000. Entry charge

Mall Galleries: www.mallgalleries.org.uk, 020 7930 6844. Entry charge (free for under 16s)

Mansion House: www.cityoflondon.gov.uk and follow the links for History & Heritage/Buildings within the City/Mansion House, 020 7626 2500. Entry charge for tours

Market Porter pub: 020 7407 2495

Marks & Spencer, Marble Arch: http://www.marksandspencer.com/gp/store-locator and type in marble arch, 020 7935 7954

The Monument: www.themonument.info, 0207 626 2717. Entry charge

Mudlark pub: 020 7403 7364

Museum of London: www.museumoflondon.org.uk, 020 7001 9844. Free

Museum of London Docklands: www.museumindocklands.org.uk, 020 7001 9844. Entry charge (free for under 16s)

The Narrow pub: www.gordonramsay.com/thenarrow, 020 7592 7950

National Army Museum: www.national-army-museum.ac.uk, 020 7881 2455. Free

National Gallery: www.nationalgallery.org.uk, 020 7747 2885. Free

National Maritime Museum: www.nmm.ac.uk, 020 8858 4422. Free

National Maritime Museum's Galleries: www.nmm.ac.uk/places/maritime-galleries, 020 8858 4422. Free

National Portrait Gallery: www.npg.org.uk, 020 7306 0055. Free

National Theatre: www.nt-online.org, 020 7452 3400

Natural History Museum: www.nhm.ac.uk, 020 7942 5000. Free

Old Curiosity Shop: www.curiosityuk.com, 020 7405 9891

Old Royal Naval College: www.oldroyalnavalcollege.org, 020 8269 4747. Free

Open Air Theatre, Regent's Park: www.openairtheatre.org, 08443 753 460

Oratory of St Philip Neri, Brompton: www.bromptonoratory.com, 020 7808 0900

Oxo Tower Restaurant: www.harveynichols.com/output/Page128.asp, reservations 020 7803 3888

Paxton & Whitfield, Cheesemongers: www.paxtonandwhitfield.co.uk and follow the link for Our Shops, 020 7930 0259

Peter Jones: www.peterjones.co.uk, 020 7730 3434